Care For prisoners And Their Families In The North East

1882-2007

The Story of NEPACS

Ruth Cranfield

ISBN 978-0-9530187-4-1

Design & Layout: Paul Forrest (*www.alsdesign.co.uk)*
Production Editor: Martyn McFadden
Proof Reading: Sheila Seacroft

Contents

Preface

The Durham Discharged Prisoners' Aid Society has been reprehensibly careless of its archives, and has preserved little evidence of its own past. Happily, however, its officials honoured their obligation to send copies of the reports to the central body, and in this way most of the annual reports for the years 1916-1963 have been preserved, and may be consulted in the Modern Records Centre of the University of Warwick. We must be grateful, too, to past editors of the Durham County Advertiser who printed very full accounts of the annual meetings of the Society for most years until the middle of the twentieth century, and to the libraries which make it possible for these to be read. The annual reports and the Advertiser were my most comprehensive printed sources. The Quarter Sessions Order Books provided valuable information about the nineteenth century activities.

I would like to thank the Durham County Advertiser Management for permission to quote from past numbers of the paper. My thanks are also due to NACRO and the Modern Records Centre of Warwick University for access to the NACRO collection of DPAS reports deposited in the Centre, the Durham County Archives Department and the Durham City Branch Library for their assistance.

Information from these written sources was supplemented richly by the memories of a number of people who have been connected with the Society in this century, and I am very grateful to the following people for their willingness to talk to me and in some cases to supply printed as well as oral material about the past. Mrs Cissie Harrison and Dr Thomas Holmes, the daughter and grandson respectively of Thomas and Sarah Holmes, Mr Tom Lister, the son of Nellie and James Lister, Mrs McNamara, the widow of Mr T. McNamara, Mrs Vesta Errington, Councillor Bennie Abrahams and Mr Tom Madrell.

I must also thank Mr Alan Scott, Assistant Chief Probation Officer in Cleveland, for the original suggestion that the Society's past would be worth looking into, and for his constructive criticisms of my typescript.

Note to this edition
I must add my thanks to the many people who helped with Part II, particularly those who figure in it and were invited to comment on parts of the text. The mistakes remain my own. I am also very grateful to Kath Simpson for her most useful help with the illustrations and to everyone who encouraged the effort, especially to Sheila Seacroft for her great help in seeing the manuscript through the press.

R.C.

PART I

One hundred years of Prisoners' Aid in County Durham

1882-1982

1.   ORIGINS AND PRECURSORS

For many of the prisoners who passed through the gates of a Victorian gaol, the prospect before them as they left the prison was far more chilling than when they had entered it. For, while the worst horrors and the dreadful filth and miasma of the eighteenth century gaols had for the most part been eradicated, the attitude of Victorian society, complacent, censorious and unimaginative, created an environment in which the person who had once broken the law found it virtually impossible to keep himself alive without breaking it again.

The prisoner released from Durham Gaol probably turned his steps towards the crowded slums of New Elvet, where he would be less conspicuous than in the elegant and spacious Old Elvet, lined with the town houses of the gentry and professional classes. Possibly he planned to tramp to one of the ports along the coast where work on a ship was fairly easy to come by, or to one or other of the collieries where jobs were plentiful and not too many questions would be asked. In respect of employment opportunities, indeed, the discharged prisoner in County Durham was among the more fortunate of his kind, especially in the thriving days of railway building and the expanding coal and metal industries of the mid-century.

But the immediate future presented pressing problems. What could he eat? Where could he sleep? He might have a small amount of money in his possession, given him by the authorities to assist him on his journey, but, when that was gone, as it quickly would be, destitution faced him unless he had already found a job. Then it was likely to be a choice between resorting to theft or perishing of hunger. As Archdeacon Hamilton put it at the end of the century, looking back to the forties: "No one looked after them, and there were many who left prison without a hat or a coat, or without shoes, and that with perhaps six or eight inches of snow on the ground. Now the real question placed before a fellow creature in such a predicament was – shall I starve or steal?"[1]

If the outlook was bleak for a male prisoner, it was many times worse for a female. Her character was gone and her reputation blackened. She was not only a 'gaol bird' but also a 'fallen woman'. No decent house would open its door to her, so the path to service was blocked. Every pressure of society drove her towards a low lodging-house, where she was likely to sink still lower, or on to the streets, or to the ships lying in dock at the seaports.

---
[1] *Durham County Advertiser, 12.2.1892*

Both men and women coming out of prison could expect to find a warmer welcome, more practical assistance and more concern for their future among their old, or new, criminal associates - a situation which made their drift back into crime, whatever good intentions they had formed, almost inevitable. This was true as much for the first offender – possibly only on the very fringe of crime, possibly even innocent of the offence for which he had been sentenced – as for the hardened law-breaker. Once marked by the stigma of gaol a person became an outcast from 'respectable' society, and likely to be driven deeper and deeper into the criminal sub-culture which teemed with vitality in the 'rookeries' of every well-populated town.

From the late eighteenth century, however, some efforts had been made in different parts of the country, to provide more hopeful alternatives for discharged prisoners, by philanthropists who recognized the tragedy of their situation, and formed societies with the purpose of offering them assistance. In 1862, Parliament acknowledged that Discharged Prisoners' Aid Societies had "been formed in divers parts of England, by persons subscribing voluntarily, for the purpose of finding employment for discharged prisoners, and enabling them by loans and grants of money to live by honest labour," [2] and authorized magistrates to pay each society a sum of money, not exceeding £2 for each prisoner released, to be used for the benefit of discharged prisoners, so granting them official recognition.

In Durham, although no formal society appeared as yet, the middle years of the century witnessed a considerable amount of positive activity on behalf of those leaving prison. Though a project for establishing a refuge to receive discharged prisoners from the gaols of Newcastle, Durham and Northumberland, which was being considered by a committee of magistrates in 1843, [3] appears to have foundered, probably because of financial difficulties, a refuge system for Durham prisoners had been brought into being before the end of the decade. It was the work of the well-known reforming Chaplain of Durham Gaol, the Rev. George Hans Hamilton. Repudiating the notion of a visible institution labelled 'Durham Refuge for Discharged Prisoners' as liable to create more embarrassments than it would solve, he developed a scheme which made provision for those prisoners whose intentions were good and whose needs genuine. Thus, men and boys who were willing to go to sea were sent to Sunderland (they had to walk there as a test of their good intentions), where arrangements had been made with a shipping agent who would give them lodging in his house until he could get them employed or bound apprentice, and sent to sea; while those who were

---

[2] 25 & 26 Vict., c.44
[3] Durham Quarter Sessions Order Book, 1843. DCRO Q/S/OB 26.

resolved to find employment inland would be maintained in respectable lodgings while they applied to the pits, the carpet manufactory, or elsewhere. Girls who qualified for aid were accommodated in the assistant schoolmaster's house, where they were engaged in knitting and sewing and learning useful skills until they could be placed in service. Hamilton overcame much of the reluctance to employ such fallen females by employing one in his own home, and by ensuring that they were instructed in housework and deportment. By such means as these, 132 discharged prisoners were assisted during the year 1852 at a cost to the Refuge of £71.13s.4d. In addition, the Chaplain and the managers of the Refuge were able to arrange for 97 young prisoners to be met by their parents, or taken home at the expense of their parents or former masters. Hamilton claimed that this was the first such Refuge in the kingdom. At any rate, it was one of six listed in the Second Report of the Reformatory and Refuge Union in 1858. The zeal of the good Chaplain had initiated an effective scheme which, by the application of common-sense, humanity, and a considerable amount of industry, was evidently successful in opening doors to independence and respectability for a substantial number of offenders. Of the 1093 prisoners dealt with in the six years, 1848-54, at the cost of £391.07.03, apparently only 129 failed to make good.[4]

During the same period, and partly at the instigation of Hamilton, supported by Dean Waddington and Rowland Burdon, a Penitentiary was established by public subscription, to receive some of the most destitute and forsaken women and girls on their discharge. In the grey stone building on the north side of Gilesgate, Durham, now known as Kepier House, the inmates underwent a rigorous regime of hard work and spare diet, which, if they persevered, as not all of them did, fitted most of them to find and keep some form of employment – usually service in a private house.

While the penitentiary, founded by public subscription, became the recipient of a number of substantial bequests which placed it in a secure financial position, the refuge, remaining more or less anonymous, was maintained by the contributions of a group of voluntary donors whom Hamilton had gathered into an informal society, following his appeal to the magistrates in 1849:"If, however, a few philanthropic gentlemen of the county were to form themselves into a committee for the purpose of quietly placing reformed and improved prisoners in positions far from temptations and at a distance from their bad companions

---

[4] *This paragraph is largely based on Hamilton's evidence included in the* Report from the Select Committee on Criminal and Destitute Children, *1853.*

then a greater amount of good might be effected and considerable expense saved."[5]

But the arrangement was highly personal, dependent on Hamilton's association among the local clergy and gentry, and after his departure from Durham in 1854 the 'society' and its work seem to have dissolved as quietly as they had come into being.

The responsibility for assisting discharged prisoners was left once more entirely to the Chaplains, some of whom took this aspect of their duties very seriously. The Refuge system seems to have been maintained, and there was still some money available, from both official and unofficial sources, for expending on fares, tools, clothes and other items which would assist the discharged prisoners in efforts to retrieve their characters. The Penitentiary survived, well-endowed and financially robust, but unattractive to many of those for whose benefit it had been established: "Among the female prisoners", the Chaplain, the Rev. J.C.Lowe, reported in 1875, "there prevails a most decided aversion to all Penitentiaries."[6]

Meanwhile, as we have seen, the Discharged Prisoners' Aid Societies were winning official recognition, and in 1874 a plan was mooted at the Durham County Quarter Sessions for the formation of a Durham Society, and a committee appointed. The Chairman of the County Bench, John Lloyd Wharton, was very keen, and spoke enthusiastically about the work of the Stafford Discharged Prisoners' Aid Society, observing that the work was not supported by county funds, but by voluntary subscriptions, and that very few prisoners who had received assistance from the Society there had relapsed into criminal ways. But Wharton was a man of many interests, and when the newly appointed secretary, a former Chaplain at Durham Prison, currently Rector of St Mary's parish, Shincliffe, the Rev. George Robert Bulman was forced to be absent from Durham for a long period, the idea fell into abeyance. In January 1879, when the Home Secretary enquired about aid to discharged prisoners, Wharton had to admit that "the assistance given to prisoners was little more than nominal at Durham".[7]

When responsibility for the administration of the local prisons had passed to the Home Secretary by virtue of the Prisons Act of 1877 which created the Board of Prison Commissioners, the local magistrates had lost their power to regulate

---

[5] *Durham Quarter Sessions Order Book, 1849. DCRO Q/S/OB 27*
[6] *Durham Quarter Sessions Order Book, 1875. DCRO Q/S/OB 32*
[7] *Durham Quarter Sessions Order Book, 1879. DCRO Q/S/OB 33*

the prison existence of those who had been sentenced by them and their colleagues. The transfer of authority, together with the active interest in after-care taken by the Prison Commissioners (who discovered that the aid societies had become so inactive that the average amount disbursed on a prisoner was not more than sevenpence, although £2 was available), appears to have stimulated interest in the Discharged Prisoners' Aid Society movement, for the number of local societies more than doubled in the ten years after 1878, rising from twenty-nine to sixty-three.

Among the new societies was the one which was at last officially established in Durham in June 1882, through the efforts of Hans Hamilton, who in this year returned to Durham as Archdeacon of Northumberland and Canon Residentiary of Durham, John Lloyd Wharton, Percival Spearman Wilkinson of Mount Oswald, and the Rev. Arthur Duncombe Shafto, Rector of Brancepeth.

The effectiveness of such a society's work would be largely dependent on its financial resources. Uncertainty about the amount which could be relied on from voluntary sources had contributed substantially to the delay in forming the Society. Clearly the government grant to which the Society became entitled by virtue of the certificate of recognition which it received from the magistrates in Quarter Sessions in June 1882,[8] and which consisted of a portion of the total grant of £4,000 which was at this time allocated for sharing among all the Discharged Prisoners' Aid Societies, would not by itself be sufficient for effective work, and would have to be supplemented from other sources. The timely discovery of a number of ancient bequests whose funds could legitimately be applied to the purpose of assisting discharged prisoners had removed the last doubts, and encouraged the founders to go forward.

The most substantial of these bequests was that of Dr Thomas Wood, a seventeenth century Prebendary of Durham, later Bishop of Lichfield and Coventry, who, on his death in 1692, left land at Eaglescliffe to his nephew, with the proviso that £20 should be paid annually from the rent to the city of Durham "to be employed and disposed of towards the release of poor prisoners for debt committed to the common gaol when each such prisoner's debt did not exceed £5." Since the numbers of such debtors had become very small by the nineteenth century, and there were none at all after 1865 when a Bankruptcy Act largely abolished imprisonment for debt, a considerable sum of money had accumulated in this charitable fund. Permission was now obtained from the

---

[8] *Durham Quarter Sessions Order Book, 1882. DCRO Q/S/OB 33*

Durham Court of Chancery, on the grounds that the original purposes of the bequest had become obsolete and that the intentions of the pious founder would be fulfilled if the change were made, to transfer the administration of the money to "a certain Society called the Prisoners' Aid Society in the County of Durham", whose aim was "to assist prisoners who had been discharged from gaol to get an honest livelihood."[9]

Similar decisions secured for the Society the proceeds from the legacy of Dr William Hartwell, Rector of Stanhope and Prebendary of the Cathedral, who, by his will of 1724, left £20 to be used annually for the benefit of insolvent debtors (preference to be given to those from Stanhope), and small amounts from the bequest of John Frankelyn of Cocken, who, in 1572, willed money to provide twelvepence every Sunday for ever to poor prisoners in meat and drink, and from William Wall, whose will, dated 1679, charged his property in and about Bishop Auckland with the payment of fifteen shillings per annum to the poor prisoners in Durham Gaol.[10]

These testamentary sources were augmented by money from another modest fund, which had accrued from subscriptions paid by magistrates for the purpose of providing overnight accommodation for themselves when the business of Sessions required their attendance on two successive days, but which had not been greatly used. This money was now paid over to the new Society, and invested in preference stock. When all the funds were taken into account, the Society could count on an income of £100 a year.[11]

From the beginning, the Society had substantial, if narrowly based, support. Among its funding members were many of the county magistrates and clergy. The leading families of the county were well represented. The Marquess of Londonderry was a patron, and the Bishop of Durham President. John Lloyd Wharton, who was M.P. for Durham City from 1871 till 1874, and for the West Riding of Yorkshire from 1886 till 1906, was Vice-President. The first executive committee consisted of P.S.Wilkinson, John Shields, of Western Lodge, and Major Rowlandson, of the College, who was Treasurer.

---

[9] Report of Durham Court of Chancery in Durham County Advertiser, 13.10.1882.

[10] For much of the information in this paragraph I am indebted to C.M.Carlton, History of the charities in the city of Durham 1872. The small charities were formed into the Durham Consolidated Prison Charities in 1890.

[11] Durham County Advertiser, 23.02.1883.

2. THE EARLY YEARS, 1882-1895

As it turned out, the establishment of a financial basis had been a simpler task than applying the funds to help prisoners proved to be.

An Agent to advise the prisoners, and to maintain contact with them after they had left the prison was appointed in 1883 at a salary of £30 per annum. He was Mr Thompson Smith, of Church Street, who had retired from the office of chief warder of Durham Prison after forty years in prison service. Fitted by character and experience for the work, he evidently carried it out zealously, "in a spirit of benevolence, guided by a judgment trained by the long experience of prisoners."[12] When he retired five years later, there were only two applicants for the post. Mark Lawson, a former police sergeant, was appointed, and through his contacts with his former professional colleagues was able to extend the area of his activity. When a man was sent to the sea-ports to look for work, Lawson asked the heads of police in those towns to find him suitable board and lodging for which the Society paid, while he looked for a job. If the local police reported any flagging in the search for work, the supply of lodgings money would be cut off. One can understand that this system might prove unattractive to the released prisoner, anxious to experience his freedom untrammeled by shades of prison and police, but nevertheless it seems clear that a number of police officers in various parts of the county did take a genuinely kind and benevolent interest in the resettlement of discharged prisoners.

Most of the prisoners, however, held aloof, rather in the spirit of Arthur Morrison's Josh Perrott (in *A child of the Jago*, 1896): "He had successfully run the gauntlet of Prisoners' Aid Societies and the like, professing to have a 'job waiting for him' in Shoreditch, and his way across London had been freely punctuated at public-houses; for his prison gratuity was a very pleasant and useful little sum." The Durham prisoners, too, in the main preferred the company of their criminal associates to that of the Society's Agent. The will to reform was not often present, or at any rate strong enough to withstand the lure of the public house or the beershop. The females were worse than the males, the prison matron reporting that there were very few women prisoners who desired aid to lead a better life. The help which the Society offered, then, attracted only a lukewarm response. Assistance was offered in finding work, but many prisoners preferred to find their own. The shelter of the Penitentiary or other similar homes or refuges was rejected by women who found their discipline repellent and reformation

---

[12] *Durham County Advertiser, 07.03.1884.*

daunting. The prisoners wanted money gifts without strings, and these the Society was rarely prepared to give. Even small pecuniary gifts, it found, could be misused. A widow, for example, who was met on her release by officials from the Union bringing her children, and was given five shillings for food, was found the same night helplessly drunk, and returned to prison. This woman's massive problems were, of course, far beyond the reach of the Society to solve with the slight means at its disposal. Her case illustrates the fundamental fact that the disproportion between the dimensions of the need and those of the aid available perpetually bedevilled the Society's good intentions.

Members, recognizing their weakness and yet convinced that "the action of societies such as theirs tended to the diminution of crime" explored the possible causes for failure. There was a good bit of truth in the analysis suggested by P.S.Wilkinson in the annual report for 1886 – at a time when the number of prisoners had decreased – that the majority of prisoners belonged to the confirmed criminal class, and, having no desire for amendment, would not seek the Society's aid, while most of the exceptions to that rule had homes to return to and did not need their help. The view that Durham County produced a particularly intractable type of prisoner persisted. Wharton lamented in 1888, that "in the gaol at Durham they had about as awkward a class of people to deal with as any in the country, especially the women."[13] Colonel Armstrong, who retired from the office of Governor in 1890, believed that "the population of this county was such that we should find very few persons suitable for or seeking aid", while the incoming Governor, Mr Cruikshank, was struck by "the absence from our prison of the class of prisoners to whom assistance is most useful."[14] Yet if the ex-prisoners were disappointing, so too, in many respects, was the aid. It would take much more than a little cash, or a suit of working clothes, or even a few nights lodging to set these clients on the road to respectability. For them, as for many of their contemporaries, the times were altogether out of joint.

The committee concluded that their work could not be satisfactorily done by establishing contact at the prison gate. The only chance of implanting a firm desire for amendment of life was by counselling the prisoner while he was still serving his sentence, undistracted by the tawdry glamour and slipshod morals of low life. Permission was therefore sought to send visitors into the prison, who would try to turn the minds of inmates towards reform, and particularly for the admission of lady visitors, as in the old pre-Prison Commission days, to the females, but the Governor (Colonel Armstrong) was unwilling. Discouraged, W.H.Richardson, a county magistrate, complained in 1885 that "he regarded

---

[13]*Durham County Advertiser,02.02.1888.*
[14]*Durham County Advertiser, 30.01.1891.*

our prison system as an undoubted failure. Men and women sent to prison seemed to be worse after leaving prison than before, and that was specially true in regard to women." [15]

Since the authorities remained for the time being adamant on the subject of visitors, the Society adopted the expedient, which was acceptable to the Governor and the Commissioners, of displaying a notice in every cell, to draw the objects of the Society to the attention of those whom it hoped to help. The original wording which was provided by the central Committee of Discharged Prisoners' Aid Societies, proved to be open to misunderstanding, but a notice revised by the Durham Committee which appeared in the cells during 1889, was found more satisfactory. It ran: "Prisoners who are resolved to live respectably, and earn their own living by honest labour when discharged from prison, are informed that this society is ready to give to prisoners who are recommended by the Governor, suitable aid to assist them in carrying out their good resolutions."

Very soon after the notices had been brought into use, authority relented, and Mrs Lake, wife of the Dean of Durham, obtained permission to visit selected female prisoners, which she did on behalf of the Society. She was joined within the year by Mrs King. [16]

---

[15] *Durham County Advertiser, 10.04.1885.*
[16] *The prison visiting begun by Mrs Fry and her companions in the second decade of the nineteenth century had not become an established practice though visiting did take place occasionally. In the mid-nineteenth century, for example, when Hamilton was Chaplain of Durham Prison, a number of highly respected ladies paid regular Sunday visits. The Prison Commissioners, under their first Chairman, Colonel Sir Edmund Du Cane, appear to have permitted some visiting, and Mrs King, who was apparently in the habit of visiting even before her official appointment in 1890, must have been one of the earliest of these Lady Visitors. She was joined a few years later by Mrs Simey, and in 1903 by Mrs Alan Hutchinson, Mrs Bayley and Mrs Rogerson.*
A bold, but successful, experiment begun by the Governor, Colonel Hales in 1922, allowed the ladies to visit the young male prisoners in their cells, and it was thought that Mrs Salvin was possibly the first lady in England to visit in this way. (Durham County Advertiser, 03.04.1925.) This visiting by ladies seems from the start to have been regarded as a function of the Discharged Prisoners' Aid Society, and during the 1920s the Lady Visitors appear to have been constituted as a sub-committee of the Society. This arrangement persisted as long as there were females to be visited in Durham Prison.
In 1924 Mrs Hutchinson, who had been a visitor for twenty-one years, said that she thought the time had come for the men to share in prison visiting. "No work in the world equalled it", she said,"and prison visiting helped to keep alive faith in human goodness." The National Association of Prison Visitors had been founded in 1924 and a Durham Association came into being before long for the male visitors. They were represented on the Committee of the Prisoners' Aid Society, but the connection was not so close as it was in the case of the females.

Both these ladies were connected with the Durham Diocesan Association for the Care of Friendless Women and Girls which, in 1890, established in Framwellgate, Durham, a new refuge for females, St Catherine's Home, which was run along rather less forbidding lines than the Penitentiary. It was not intended primarily for delinquents, but for females in moral danger, but it did take a few 'prison cases', selected as suitable and persuaded to enter by Mrs King, and paid for by the Discharged Prisoners' Aid Society. Women and girls leaving the prison could now be placed, if they were willing, in the Penitentiary or St Catherine's Home or a respectable lodging-house run by a Mrs Young, who had helped the Society in this way for a few years. None of these havens proved attractive to many of the females, but each of them offered friendship, tolerance and concern, and paved the way to reform and rehabilitation for a few.

During its first ten years, then, the Durham Discharged Prisoners' Aid Society, engaged in working out its identity and its role, had encountered many frustrations. The great gulf which separated the Society's members from its clients made its work all but impossible. Mistrust and suspicion were mutual. Many of the recipients of the Society's charity were ready to bite the hands which fed them, while the Society was alacritous in rebuffing all but the most repentant and docile prisoners. Nevertheless, a little progress had been made. The Agents, working-class men themselves, were much better able to communicate with the ex-prisoners than the educated and wealthy elite who sat on the Society's committee, and the lady visitors were eliciting a positive response from some of the females. Some prisoners had been restored to their families, some had been established in employment, some, even among the recalcitrant females, had been found accommodation, and some who had accepted aid had been successfully rehabilitated.

A beginning had been made too, in establishing links with people engaged in the same kind of task in the populous towns and ports of the county. In Sunderland, which was regarded as a forcing-bed for crime, a Police Court Missionary[17] had for many years attended the courts daily, interviewing and counselling prisoners before they set off for Durham Gaol, meeting them on discharge and attempting to turn them away from criminal courses. Recently, a committee had been set

---

[17] Police Court Missionaries had appeared during the last quarter of the nineteenth century, at first as unofficial benevolent individuals (often members of the Church of England Temperance Society) who attended the magistrates courts with the intention of offering help to destitute offenders, with a view to their restoration and reclamation. They came to be accepted as useful and valuable workers, and proved to be the fore-runners of the twentieth–century probation officers.

up there to support and maintain this work, and during 1892 the members of this committee consented to act as a committee of the Durham Discharged Prisoners' Aid Society. Negotiations were opened with a similar body in Gateshead. The later Governors were enthusiastic in support of the Society, and, in 1896, Captain Frith went off to Stockton with P.S. Wilkinson to try to establish a Police Court Mission there. They were not able to stir up sufficient local support, but similar efforts were more successful in establishing Missions in Hartlepool, Stockton, Darlington, Bishop Auckland, Jarrow and South Shields.

(Left) **George Hans Hamilton, by C. W. Watson.**
By kind permission of the National Portrait Gallery

(Right) **Thomas & Sarah Holmes**
By kind permission of the family

3   "A NEW ERA". 1895-1918

In 1895 the Report of the Departmental Committee on Prisons (the Gladstone Report) presented a fundamental reappraisal of penal policy, and of official attitudes to the after-care of prisoners. The Committee condemned the prison system for treating prisoners too much as "irreclaimable criminals", instead of as men and women who could be reformed and reclaimed. Their belief that prisoners could, through careful discipline and training, be "turned out of prison better men and women physically and morally than when they came in", and that rehabilitation of the offender was a responsibility shared by the penal system and society generally, led to the conclusion that prison treatment and after-care were parts of a single process. As a consequence the Prison Commissioners began to pay more attention to the Prisoners' Aid Societies (the sole agents of after-care), which had been found by the Committee to exhibit a wide variation in standards, methods and efficiency, and the Rev. G.P.Merrick, Chaplain of Holloway Prison, was despatched on a tour of inspection of their work. He visited Durham in 1896, with a list of sixty suggestions, which the Society duly studied. New standards and regulations were now laid down by the Home Office, to which aid societies must conform in order to qualify for the Secretary of State's certificate of efficiency, which entitled them to receive the government grant. This certificate was received by the Durham Society on May 20th, 1898, signifying that it was a properly constituted and efficiently organized society.[18]

This year was felt to mark the beginning of a new era in the history of the Society. Reconstructed and revivified, with greater assurance born of the new official interest and approval, with a number of changes in personnel and an extension of the area of its endeavours, it moved forward vigorously into a decade which was to witness enlargement of the volume of its work and the adoption of new methods in the treatment of criminals.

Durham County was, around the turn of the century, one of the most populous counties in Britain, its inhabitants being largely concentrated in the densely peopled industrial towns and sea-ports in the east. Its heavy industries – shipbuilding, coal and iron – attracted numerous non-native, often transient workers, and its position on the easiest route between Scotland and southern England brought in large numbers of migrants, tramps and other wayfarers. Such restless and rootless inhabitants as these were particularly defenceless

---

[18] *Durham County Advertiser, 10.02.1899*

against both temptation and accusation. They were far away from the restraints of childhood neighbours and family; they were outside, rather than in, the community, isolated among natives; they were prone to seek their only comfort in the public houses; as strangers they were easily blamed, and in a crisis they had no one to whom they could turn for help. Not surprisingly, they were frequently in trouble with the law. At any rate, for one reason or another, the county regularly achieved the unwelcome distinction of having the highest crime rate in the country. The more integrated members of the population were keenly aware of the threats to the order and stability of their society, not to mention the security of their property, which this high rate of criminality posed, and looked askance at the ex-prisoner, whether native or new-comer.

Members of the Discharged Prisoners' Aid Society in this context saw a double purpose in their work: the establishment of individual criminals in a better way of life, and the protection of the local community from the increase of criminality. They knew that a large proportion of the inmates of the prison were not natives of Durham, and worried about the effects of "Durham's deluge of bad characters" as large numbers of prisoners were discharged at the expiry of their sentences into the city and county. When it is considered that, in 1900, 6,179 prisoners were discharged into a population of one million, it is easy to understand the eagerness with which they were encouraged to board their trains and disperse to their own homes. The Society saw its mission, then, as primarily philanthropic, in extending aid to society's outcasts, but also as public-spirited in the sense that, by redeeming the criminal, it was reducing the amount of crime, and thus the cost of maintaining prisoners in gaol, and, by dispersing the prisoners, it was safeguarding the local community.

This being so, members felt justified in expecting support from the city and county, and aggrieved that interest was so difficult to awaken, and that, in one of the wealthiest counties in the United Kingdom, subscriptions were so hard to get. A perennial cause of annoyance was the slenderness of the contributions from the flourishing seaports and busy towns, whose denizens were costing the Society dearly. "The people in the large towns, really responsible for most of the crime, know scarcely anything of the Society", the Chairman, Mr J.G.Hodgson complained in 1905.[19]

The results of efforts to spread information and win support were disappointing. In 1904, the Chairmen of all the Petty Sessions in the County and the Mayors

---

[19] *Durham County Advertiser, 03.03.1905.*

of the Boroughs were added to the General Committee, and seven hundred copies of the Annual Report were distributed, but with little effect on either the attendance at meetings or the receipts from subscriptions. Apathy, misunderstanding and suspicion frustrated such ventures. People seemed to think that the Society gave doles and help to all prisoners on discharge, lamented Mr Hodgson. "Nothing", he claimed indignantly, "could be further from the truth."[20]

The truth was, of course, that only carefully sifted prisoners were offered aid, and then they were closely supervised by the Agent. The new Agent, appointed by the Society in 1898 to succeed Mark Lawson, contributed perhaps more than anyone to the building up of its credibility and effectiveness. Appointed at a salary of £100 per annum to carry out the increased duties arising from the regulations of the Home Office, Thomas Holmes[21] soon established a routine which included visiting in their cells all prisoners with sentences of at least a month, seeing every prisoner on the morning of his discharge from prison, and going to the station every day to see the released prisoners off, partly, no doubt, in order to provide moral support in their renewed encounter with a hostile world, but partly also to ensure that the tickets issued to ex-prisoners were used to transport their holders away from Durham, and not bartered for the price of a drink. He would also try to sever links which had been formed in prison between criminals, and to break up old damaging associations.

In Holmes, the Society had an Agent whose disposition, experience and abilities, and whose knowledge of places and people were excellently suited to the work, and who from the first showed judgment and discretion of a very high order. Unlike his predecessors, he had no previous connection with prison or police, but his life as a railway fitter had given him an understanding of the working world into which he was for ever trying to fit his charges, and he well perceived the difficulties, the stresses, the suspicions and temptations that they would encounter in it. In his youth a celebrated Cumberland wrestler and in maturity a keen and first-class gardener, he applied to all aspects of his life a patient thoroughness and an austere persistence which could not fail to impress. Kind of heart and generous by nature, he attracted the trust of many of the men, while at the same time he demanded their honest cooperation, and commended to them the high moral principles which governed his own life.

---

[20] *Durham County Advertiser, 19.03.1909.*
[21] *For more information about Thomas and Sarah Holmes, see my article, "Thomas and Sarah Holmes" p.95, in Durham County Local History Society Journal, No 72, May 2007.*

He was a church-goer and a lay-preacher, and, as a teetotaler, he frequently persuaded the men whom he was hoping to rehabilitate to sign the pledge. At a time when nearly all observers agreed that a very large amount of crime was directly attributable to excessive drinking – in 1902 the committee of the Society blamed 91% of all prison sentences in Durham on drunkenness – this was a very pertinent endeavour.

The good results of Holmes's work were observed and commended by the Society. They were partly, perhaps, due to the fact that among the prison population were many men who could be described as "accidental criminals", those who were law-breakers neither by training nor inclination, but who had fallen foul of the law through a single misdemeanour, through the poverty or misfortune of their situation, or through acquaintance with an habitual delinquent. Such people, particularly if they were first offenders, were very likely to get from Holmes the help that they needed to overcome their past and reform their lives. Many of them, while not receiving financial assistance and therefore not appearing in the statistics, yet received practical help and advice in matters, as the Chaplain put it in 1900, of "daily life, trade, labour and domestic economy"; some found their homes and their marriages saved by his intervention. Evidence of the efficacy of his work was seen in the many grateful letters, "written tokens of love and gratitude", which he received from ex-prisoners. He, on his part, gave extended encouragement by continuing to write to some of those who had been successfully rehabilitated.

For a time he laboured among the women too, doing what he could, but it was obvious that this work would be better done by a female, and, in 1900, his wife, Sarah, was appointed Assistant Agent at a salary of £20 a year. She was a woman of stalwart personality, shrewd, upright, something of a martinet, tough and firm – well-fitted to deal with the wayward females, the despair of all who tried to do them good, who passed through the prison. Some of these she did motivate to change their way of life, and, like her husband, she maintained a supportive correspondence with many whom she had helped. She, too, tried to persuade the women to sign the pledge before leaving the prison, in the knowledge that drunkenness was the downfall of women even more than of men. (On a visit to one public house in the county during 1920 the police found nearly one hundred women on the premises.)

It is clear that Colonel Wisden, the Prison Governor, had good grounds for saying, in 1917, that Mr and Mrs Holmes were the envy of other societies. They remained with the Society until 1921, acting also as the first Probation Officers for the county, appointed under the Probation of Offenders Act of 1908. One of their sons, Thomas, joined the Durham County Constabulary in 1920, was Chairman of the Police Federation of England and Wales from 1931-34 and became Detective Superintendent at the head of Durham's C.I.D. in 1939. When they left the Society's employment they continued to work as Probation Officers until 1928. In 1921, they were succeeded as the Society's Agents by their son-in-law and daughter, Nellie and James Lister. Before they left home, the two sons and three daughters had all contributed to the running of the Refuge, for Thomas and Sarah Holmes regarded the family atmosphere as an important rehabilitating factor.

The enterprise of Thomas and Sarah was supported by an invigorated Society. The new official status and the approval of the Home Office, which now looked to such societies to carry out work which it acknowledged to be an integral part of the penal system, together with the friendly cooperation of the Governors, had opened the prison gates to them, and the sub-committee which considered the cases of the individual prisoners now sat in the prison, at first weekly, and then, from 1900, twice a week. The number of cases dealt with rose substantially. Many were passed on to the numerous local Agents who now operated nearly all over the county, usually financed by the voluntary effort of their own locality, but working in cooperation with the Durham committee, and supported by voluntary helpers, by the Salvation Army, the local clergy of many denominations and the police.

At this time, the police officers of all ranks, superintendents, inspectors and sergeants, were counted among the best friends of the Society, working sympathetically with the Agents, helping in the hunt for jobs, especially for the young, on whom they frequently kept a friendly eye. Colonel Darwin, Chairman of the Society, commented in 1914: "In many cases prisoners found their best friends in a police sergeant."[22] The Chief Constable, W.G.Morant, was a regular attender at committee meetings, and used his connections at South Shields to find a competent man to act as Agent there. By telling a few of his friends about the Society he raised a sum of £20 for it. His wife was an active member of the ladies' committee, and a prison visitor for many years. Her warm and sympathetic nature endeared her not only to the girls in St Mary's Home as the old Penitentiary had come to be called, but also to "her beloved policemen", as she called the members of her husband's Force.

---

[22] *Durham County Advertiser, 20.03.1914.*

The Governors, too, were generous with their assistance and support. With the passing of the county prisons into the control of the Prison Commissioners (1877), there came a national system of staff appointments, and consequently a rapid turnover of men, frequently of army background, in the course of promotion. Those who came to Durham seem mostly to have been humane and magnanimous, and to have welcomed the Society's activities. Captain Frith (1897-99) wanted to see a higher proportion of prisoners receiving aid, and he entered with zest into the endeavour to increase the number of Police Court Missionaries. His successors, Captain Burgoyne and Captain Farrant, continued to look for suitable cases among the prisoners and attended committee meetings. Mr Dillon (1907-08), believing that "without such societies he did not know what the work of prison officials would be", was himself, he averred, "almost prepared to say he would go into debt to meet the demands made on the Society."[23]

Help came also from employers, willing to take on men proposed by the Society, and from the families of the men themselves. Magistrates, judges and sheriffs supported and approved. Judge Francis Greenwell never tired of praising the Society. In 1911, Mr Justice Grantham, addressing the Grand Jury at the summer Assizes, reminded them that it was almost impossible for a convicted person to get back again into his old position in life by his own efforts, and that the Discharged Prisoners' Aid Society was the only means by which he could attain respectability again. This was an apposite reminder since by now it had become customary to take a collection amongst the Grand Jury for the Society's funds.

Like all responsible bodies, official and unofficial, concerned with questions of crime and punishment, the Society was deeply troubled by juvenile crime and the treatment of juvenile offenders. It had long been felt that assisting the young prisoners on discharge was perhaps the most significant area of the Society's work. Members were keenly interested in the development from 1902 onwards of Borstal Training as an imaginative and hopeful method of dealing with young law-breakers. By 1906 a "modified Borstal system" was operating in Durham Prison, involving a new regime of training and discipline. With a carpenter's shop, and a blacksmith's shop, and, from 1910, instruction in needlework for the girls, as well as lectures from local gentlemen on a variety of subjects, the young inmates were offered a practical training in useful skills which it was hoped would later equip them to find and keep employment. The Society, acting on recommendations of the Prison Commissioners, formed a special Borstal Committee, which was almost identical with the committee of the Discharged

---

[23] *Durham County Advertiser, 13.03.1908.*

Prisoners' Aid Society itself, with the addition of the Lady Visitors, and which was prepared to make special efforts to save juvenile offenders from becoming established in criminal careers. Thomas and Sarah acted inside and outside the prison for both committees. There were no special funds for the Borstal work, which was financed from the Society's ordinary resources. The work of reestablishing the juveniles was time-consuming. Two members of the committee in rotation, and for a month at a time, took responsibility for ensuring that boys and girls returning to freedom had either a suitable home or an employer to receive them. The members, meeting their clients more closely than ever before, as they tried to assess their characters and aptitudes, developed new insights. They came to understand, as they strove to avoid putting square pegs into round holes, that town lads would not settle into jobs in the country, and that lads accustomed to streethawking could seldom be persuaded to get regular employment. As they searched for hopeful openings, often visiting the youths' homes, sometimes finding allies in the parents or other relations, they surely deepened their own understanding of the county in which they and their charges lived. Happily, a very positive response came from many employers, who were willing "not only to find merely the work for the lad, but to do everything that lay in their power to place him under good influences."[24] The difficulty of placing the discharged prisoners of every age naturally increased in times when employment was scarce, perhaps because of industrial disputes; but in general the committee in 1910 believed that "no really deserving young man or woman left prison without a job."[25] Now that these young offenders were undergoing systematic training in technical skills as well as the discipline of prison life, no doubt the employers recognized that an ex-prisoner was quite as likely as, even possibly more likely than, the youth who had neither prison sentence nor training, to be a good worker. Certainly, members of the Borstal Committee believed that the thorough training was largely responsible for the success which they were experiencing in their work of superintending the transition of the young prisoner to normal life. With the fervour of converts, they now wanted to extend the benefits of Borstal Training more widely, and they implored magistrates to avoid the short sentences which did nothing for the offender except remove the fear of prison, and to award longer terms of imprisonment so that young prisoners "might get the full benefit of that excellent system" (Chief Constable Morant) - and so stand a better chance of rehabilitation. To be fair, they did at the same time advocate the use of the Probation of Offenders Act (1907) as an alternative to a prison sentence. It was the short sentences often imposed for drunkenness and immorality which were so unpopular.

---

[24] *Durham County Advertiser. 02.03.1906*
[25] *Durham County Advertiser, 25.02.1910*

While these new ways of working with young prisoners were being explored, a more spirited attempt was being made to tackle the old, depressing problem of the female discharged prisoners. Most of the women had been charged with drunkenness, immorality, or neglect of their children – all three offences likely to be closely connected – and their disposal simply bristled with difficulties. If they were not to be returned to the environment which had helped to make them into criminals, and if employers would not take them straight from prison, and if they themselves remained resolutely unwilling to enter homes or penitentiaries, as most of them did, then some other half-way house would have to be provided to shelter them while they were being eased along the path to respectability. So it was that the Society, prompted, perhaps, by the resourceful Sarah Holmes, began to think seriously of obtaining premises which could provide a temporary refuge for these women at the point of greatest vulnerability, and where they could stay until they were restored to their friends or obtain employment. The Society formed a committee to study the project, which would commit them to substantial financial liabilities, but the ladies, not tarrying for any, set about finding money for a refuge, and, in 1906, raised £100 by their own efforts. The following year, the lease of 19, Old Elvet, a residence close to the prison, was secured, and Mr and Mrs Holmes moved in. Sarah was to act as Matron, under the direction of the Ladies' Committee. There was room for three women to stay in the Refuge at a time, and by the end of 1907, eighteen women had passed through it, none of whom had returned to prison, and seven of whom were known to be doing well. "Considering the class of prisoner", and the enormous difficulties these women had to face, this result was considered encouraging. The women stayed in the Refuge for days or weeks, and under the strict eye of Mrs Holmes were trained in domestic skills. Places were sought for them, and Sarah was frequently to be seen, with pony and trap, driving round the county, taking the girls for interviews or placements with one of the landed families who were willing to take them as servants.

The Refuge was homely, busy and adaptable. As well as receiving the females and some young boys on their way back to normal life, it gave breakfast to a large number of people on the morning of their release. It provided a meeting place for families and friends with released prisoners. Sometimes these families and friends coming to meet a prisoner stayed there overnight, and many of the ex-prisoners who had stayed there returned to visit on their days off, or even to spend a weekend or a few days holiday. On occasions, the Refuge served as a Remand Home, receiving people sent by the local courts to save them from the taint of prison. When there was room, Mrs Holmes would take women to help other bodies such as the Durham Rescue Workers. The building was purchased by the Society in 1919, with money donated by numerous subscribers, including most of the nobility and gentry of the county.[26]

However, as probation came to be used more regularly for the "more hopeful cases", and only the hard-core of toughened offenders were sent to prison, the Refuge came to be less frequently used, and by the late 1920s the question of its continued maintenance was being discussed. The ladies defended it, and it was reprieved.

---

[26] *Annual Report for 1919.*

4.   'THE DOLOROUS DAYS' 1919-1935

The war years, 1914-1918, placed no great strain on the Society as such. The numbers in prison, of both men and women, were low, and the discharged prisoners were more easily absorbed into the army or society on their release. The Society continued to function, but the needs of ex-prisoners were on the whole less pressing than those of the armed forces, and there were no new developments in after-care.

But the end of the war was followed by a very difficult period. Peace by no means brought about the expected return to pre-war conditions, nor did it bring plenty. After a short boom came the depressions and unemployment, which hit the north hard in the 1920s and the 1930s. In 1921 the soup kitchen in Moatside Lane, Durham, which had been established in the nineteenth century by the Mendicity Society, for use in hard times, was reopened. In that year, the new Bishop of Durham, Herbert Hensley Henson, spoke of "the moral strain and mental anxiety which had come upon thousands of honest workers in Sunderland through unemployment". In 1933, he referred to the "dolorous pre-eminence" of the county which was one of the areas most severely stricken by the Great Depression. Writing to The Times, the Bishop referred to the conditions in his diocese as "perhaps the worst in England", and said that out of every 10,000 in the population, 667 were receiving poor relief money. The heavy industries – coal-mining, shipbuilding, engineering, the iron and steel works – normally the great employers of labour in the north-east, were all badly affected, and forced to lay off thousands of their workers. Opportunities in other fields of labour contracted too. Even places in domestic service, and generally in private houses and gardens, diminished in number as employers, suffering themselves from the leanness of the times, learned to combine jobs and employ fewer servants.[27]

The physical environment in which many of the unemployed lived offered little encouragement to them in resisting temptation to crime. Inadequate housing promoted overcrowding, insanitary habits, promiscuity and violence. In Durham City, which was by no means the worst of the urban centres, there were yet terrible slums in parts of New Elvet, Hallgarth Street, and along the old main road to the north, through Milburngate and Framwellgate. Here, in narrow , dirty

---

[27] Mr Tom Lister recalls that during the thirties, when he and his mother, who was at that time the Society's Assistant Agent, were given a holiday at Unthank Hall, Haltwhistle, the home of Captain Webster, Chairman of the Society, he found one servant doing the work of two.

streets, courts and yards, decaying houses teemed with life – human, animal and insect – from cellars to attics, in rookeries as malevolent and unhealthy, if not as extensive, as those of London. In 1933, Joan Conquest, a novelist, delivered a blistering denunciation of the city, whose slums, she claimed, were the worst in the country. "Words fail me", she wrote, "in an effort to describe the horror of it all". She described a passage in Hallgarth Street, where fourteen families had to use one common tap near a foul midden, and a yard in New Elvet where a family of seven slept in one room, through whose floor a drain sometimes oozed. She found there scarcely a house with an indoor water supply, and commented on the bugs, snails, maggots and flies, rats and mice which flourished in such conditions. (It is true that she was a stranger to Durham, and something of a sensationalist, but she had written a book, *The Naked Truth*, about the London slums, had served as a nursing sister in the 1914-18 war, and was accompanied on her investigation by an N.S.P.C.C. inspector).[28] The inseparable connection noted by the Victorians, between "filth, misery, vice and crime", [29] became even closer when a fifth condition was added – idleness. It was easy for the unemployed to fall into crime. By 1927 it was observed that two thirds of the prison population had been unemployed at the time of committal to prison, and that one third had been out of work for longer than a year.

The young were especially vulnerable to unemployment. Shipbuilding and coal-mining in particular, which had provided many jobs for boys, were in difficulties from the early twenties. In 1925, the Prison Governor, Colonel H.M.A. Hales, remarked of the young prisoner: "He does not know what work is and sees no connection between it and daily bread. Two or three years ago he left school and has loafed about the streets ever since".[30] By 1933, there were more than 20,000 boys and youths unemployed in the county. Idle and bored, they wandered about the streets, ragged and often bare-footed, without interest and without prospects, showing increasing signs of undernourishment. Temptation beckoned them at every turn. The irksomeness of their empty days oppressed them. Bishop Henson noticed that the lads preferred to spend their small resources on going to the cinema or to football matches, even when this meant that they would go hungry at home. Pleasures were available for those who could pay, and this increased the temptation. An experienced police sergeant stated in 1937 that children would steal pennies to go to the cinema, and there

---

[28] *Durham County Advertise, 01.09.1919*   .
[29] *Robert Rawlinson, in a Board of Health Report, 1851. Quoted by E.N.Williams in A documentary history of England. Vol.2.1965*
[30] *Durham County Advertiser, 23.01.1925.*

see unsuitable films which gave them ideas for further misdeeds. The Young Prisoners' Committee (as the Borstal Committee of the Society was known from 1922) observed that an increasing number of boys were coming to prison through idleness.

The need in the county stimulated a number of individuals – many of them connected with the university, notably Colonel A.A.Macfarlane-Grieve, Master of University College, and Canon Edward Pace, of Hatfield College – to establish a Boys' Club, at first in a disused workshop in Back Lane, Walkergate, and then in a building in Saddler Street, Durham, made available by the Salvation Army. An American, W. Harkness, had given money to equip boys' clubs in the distressed mining areas of Durham, and additional grants were obtained from the Pilgrim Trust and the Carnegie Trust. It was not a club for delinquent boys, but for any boys who had left school and were without employment. Yet the project was very significant in the field of juvenile crime, and those who were closely involved with young offenders took a great interest in it. A public meeting held in 1933, which led to the formation of the Durham County Association of Boys' Clubs, was attended by Captain A.E.Scott, the Prison Governor, the Rev. J.J.Pigg, the Prison Chaplain, Mr J. Lister, the Discharged Prisoners' Aid Society Agent and the Chief Constable. The chief speaker was the renowned reforming Prison Commissioner, Alec Paterson, who suggested that money spent in building youth clubs to keep the young out of prison might reduce the necessity to spend it in building prison cells. Boys' clubs, indeed, could be regarded as a form of crime prevention.

For those who did offend, the Society still had the hope that they might be prevented from becoming habitual criminals. Probation was felt by many to be the best prospect. Captain Scott supposed that there was "no piece of legislation which had done more to stop young folk from entering upon anti-social courses than had that system".[31] The Discharged Prisoners' Aid Society, and others interested in prison reform, continued to implore magistrates to make more use of probation and avoid passing short custodial sentences on young offenders. If probation was judged unsuitable, fines were advocated as an alternative, though it was recognized that non-payment could easily land the youth in prison after all. Captain Scott, at the annual meeting of the Society in 1933 told members of a case of this kind, in which two boys who had been fined nine shillings and sixpence for having stolen a turnip had been unable to pay the fine and were consequently sent to prison for seven days. This was not, he said, at all an extreme example. Such short sentences were condemned by the Home

---

[31] *Durham County Advertiser, 23.01.1931.*

Office, the Prison Governors and the aid societies. They could have no reformatory effect, but might well remove for ever the salutary, deterring fear of prison, besides exposing the young person to the malevolent influence of worse criminals then himself. A short sentence was very likely to lead quickly to a second, and a third, and in the end to a life of crime. Yet in Durham, as throughout the country, boys and girls were still being sent to prison for short periods, sometimes for trivial offences, sometimes for first offences. (They would normally not be under sixteen, but occasionally younger children were imprisoned.)

Almost everyone agreed that, if a young person must go to prison, Borstal Training offered the best chance of bringing about some reformation of character. By 1931 there were four Borstal institutions in England, which took only boys who had sentences of at least two years. (The only Borstal for girls was at Aylesbury.) Boys with shorter terms remained in the prisons, and, since Durham had been designated a collecting prison for young prisoners, it received boys with sentences of between three months and two years from the whole northern area. Captain Scott had a genuine concern for, and understanding of, the offending lads, and a firm belief in their ability to reform. Although the description 'modified Borstal system' had been abandoned as misleading, he maintained a regime of training and education for the boys, whom he placed in a separate building set aside for them alone. Officers were specially selected to look after them and to give them the individual attention which Scott was convinced that they needed, and classes were run in a number of subjects by volunteers from outside the prison service. The boys' prison in Durham had remarkably good results at this time, the rate of reconviction being at least as low as that of the Borstals. It was believed that fewer than ten per cent of the boys who passed through it got into serious trouble again.

While the Borstal system had transformed the treatment of young prisoners from the first years of the twentieth century, it was not until the early 1920s, with the appointment of Alec Paterson as a Prison Commissioner, that a fundamental change in official attitudes began to produce radical reforms in the adult prisons. The Durham Discharged Prisoners' Aid Society recognized the new philosophy. "Reformation is now the key note", it was explained at the annual meeting in 1924.[32] The Prison Chaplain, R. Meiklejohn, added: "Penal work nowadays is more or less reformatory and not penal at all. The word 'penal' has all but gone". In 1929, Lieutenant-Colonel Knox, a Prison Commissioner, defined the object of imprisonment in the new terms: "…the offender would not leave prison less a

---

[32] *Durham County Advertiser, 02.05 1924.*

man, physically and mentally, than when he went in. He should be fitted to take his place in life as a citizen and not as a gaolbird..."With this end in view, the prison sought "to give a man something to think about other than crime".[33] Colonel Hales, who was Governor when the wind of change began to blow, began the liberalization of the regime and introduced some imaginative projects in adult education. Captain Scott, in the thirties, was a very fine example of the new type of prison governor, regarding reclamation as at least as important a part of his job as containment. He saw the inmates of his prison not just as prisoners, but as human beings, and, moreover, as human beings who had virtues as well as vices. He believed that only about twenty per cent of people confined in prison were habitual criminals, and that most of the others, for whom law-breaking was probably a temporary, even an accidental, state, could be prevented from returning if they received wise treatment while in prison. Treatment of offenders in prison, he believed, was very largely a preparation for their return to freedom, and he agreed with the view that the real test of a prison's effectiveness was the offender's response on discharge to the efforts that were made for his rehabilitation. The old system of punishment, he pointed out, did not keep men out of prison. He was, of course, an enthusiastic supporter of the Discharged Prisoners' Aid Society, since he regarded its work as a necessary corollary of his own, each being an interdependent part of a single whole. Convinced that the community could play an important role in reforming offenders, he was eager to keep communications open between the prison and the outside world. He himself spoke frequently at meetings throughout the county – at Rotary clubs, and public meetings, in churches and chapels – as he tried to interpret the prison world to the local population; and he appealed for volunteers, who were unconnected with the prison, to visit it to teach, for example, First Aid to the inmates (who were evidently apt pupils, for more than a hundred of them shortly won their First Aid certificates).

The effects of the more liberal prison system were certainly put to a severe test when prisoners were discharged into the world of the twenties and thirties. If the unemployed easily found their way into prison, it was by no means easy for the ex-prisoner to find employment. The task for the Society of finding work for its charges became more and more exacting. Prisoners were now interviewed on reception about their employment hopes and prospects, by the superior officers of the Prison and the Society's agent, and the information thus collected was followed up by the Society's sub-committee, meeting once or twice weekly. They kept in touch with employers, who, of course, had their own problems.

---

[33] *Durham County Advertiser, 14.02.1924.*

"We are not able yet to give employment to our own men", ran a typical letter written in 1926, this time from the second largest colliery owners in the county, "and there would be a considerable disturbance if an outsider were introduced while our own men are unemployed".[34] Even the Army and the Navy, which had in times past given many an ex-prisoner training and a career, were not now able to help. It was almost impossible to get an ex-prisoner into the armed forces, though occasionally the intervention of an influential person might lead to an exceptions' being made. In 1933, Mr Turnbull complained at the Annual Meeting of the Society that the government were the worst employers in respect of employing ex-prisoners: "The G.P.O. said that because a man had been in prison he was not a worthy citizen – not worthy to dig a hole for a telegraph pole to go into."[35] Churchmen and others were appealed to, to use their influence to persuade the government to lead the way in the matter of giving ex-prisoners a chance in life. The colonies, too, had now closed their doors to discharged prisoners. All too often, then, it proved impossible to respond positively to the heartfelt, and frequently sincere, cry of many a man and woman, "I would be alright and never come back if I could only get work".

The longer the depression lasted, the more difficult it became, not only to find work for the ex-prisoner, but also to keep alive in him a spirit willing to work. Soon the Society found it was dealing with 'corner-boys', and those who had never worked, and who would find great difficulty in accepting the discipline of a steady job. The Committee, deeply concerned about the destructive consequences of idleness, began to think that a solution might be found in the establishment of a labour colony, somewhat similar to the farm colonies already being maintained by the Salvation Army and other charitable bodies. The suggestion appealed equally to those who deplored keeping men who refused to work 'comfortable in gaol', and to those who worried about the men who were unable to find work, and the Committee resolved to prod the Home Office with a view to encouraging further development of a method which had so far been applied officially only in connection with the Industrial Schools.[36]

In spite of all their efforts, members of the Society were forced to accept that for many discharged prisoners all they could do was supply money for immediate needs until employment insurance money could be obtained. This placed extra burdens on financial resources which were already straitened through the fall

---

[34] *Annual Report for 1926.*
[35] *Durham County Advertiser,26.95.1933*
[36] *Durham County Advertiser,31.03/1927*

in subscriptions and donations consequent on the hardness of the times, and new appeals for money were made. Frequent attempts were made to gain new subscribers, and to broaden the basis of support geographically, by covering more parts of the county, and socially, by appealing to employers of labour, the Trade Unions, the Labour Party and other sections of society. There were still a good many misgivings about the Society, which was constantly accused of sentimentality and of pampering the criminal. Such accusations were vehemently denied. Members protested that there was a clear difference between those who "systematically and deliberately prey on society" and those who stumbled almost by chance into crime, or who were "temporarily crushed in the stern battle of life", who could rightly be the objects of "charitable and effective effort". Lieutenant-Colonel Knox, then Inspector of Prisons, put the case for the society with unassailable logic, when he spoke to the annual meeting in 1924. It was not simply a case, he said, of the parable of the lost sheep. "It was a form of insurance in that the man who did not get work in order to support himself would very likely become a more serious individual than a thief." Moreover, "it was financially sound. If they kept a man out of prison they saved roughly £100 per annum. It was a financial proposition because if a man could not get employment he would be receiving £1 per week whereas in prison he would be costing £2."[37]

Despite the appeals, the level of local subscribing remained low. Between 1929 and 1934 the total income from this source had shrunk by almost half. The thrice-yearly contribution of the Grand Jury was lost in 1933 when that institution was abolished by Parliament. There was never enough money, and for several years the accounts of the Society showed a deficit.

In an effort to improve the position many members of the Society engaged in fund-raising activities: for some it was just a matter of talking to wealthy friends about the Society; others appealed to the local clergy to emulate the Dean and Chapter of the Cathedral by setting aside a yearly offertory for the Society's funds; the Governors, the Chaplains and other supporters addressed public meetings; the ladies were particularly active, organising whist drives, lantern lectures and dramatic performances; and the prison staff ran a whist drive in Pattison's café in 1928, which produced £21.14.10 for the Society's funds. Bequests, such as that from Mrs Davison, a former prison officer, in 1930, which helped the Society to care specially for Gateshead prisoners, were occasionally received.

From 1921, when Mr and Mrs Holmes became full-time Probation Officers, the offices of Agent and Assistant Agent were filled by their son-in-law and

---

[37] *Durham County Advertiser 02.05.1924*

daughter, James and Nellie Lister, who had been working in Guisborough for some time as Police Court Missionaries. James Lister had been in the Church Army and, as a lay reader, continued to take services in many of the village churches round Durham. He was closely involved with the Toc H movement, and was on the committee of the Boys' Club Association. The Listers moved into 19, Old Elvet, which continued to be a port of call for prisoners leaving the gaol, who came to seek guidance, encouragement, perhaps a meal, possibly help in the search for work, or simply the small amount of money which they were entitled to expect. One frequent visitor was Emma Polkinghorne of Newcastle, who, for all her demure black-gowned appearance, served in her time well over one hundred sentences for being drunk and disorderly. Her career illustrates one of the problems which defeated both the penal and after-care services. Neither sentence nor assistance affected Emma's way of life. Any cash she received was carried promptly to the nearest chemist and there exchanged for a quantity of methylated spirits. There were many others like her, who accepted spells in prison as part of the pattern of life, and regarded themselves, on the whole, as somewhat superior to the less awkward, perhaps meeker, souls who were relegated to the workhouse. They were the despair of prison officers, penologists, reformers and Agents, who frequently begged the government to provide some method of dealing with them other than that of sending them to prison time after time for brief periods. From the Agent's point of view, one of the irritations was that, on each successive discharge, the prisoner was entitled to be clothed from the resources of the Society, which could ill afford to squander garments on these unrepentant and unappreciative characters. Commonsense and experience, however, had taught the Agents to be discriminating in their management of the clothing store.

For in these harsh times, the need for clothing assumed greater urgency, and numerous appeals were made. It was frequently found that an offender had borrowed clothing in which to come to court, in order to preserve his self-respect, and therefore he entered prison in clothes which were not his own. The Society tried to ensure that when he left prison, he had his own decent clothes, the lack of which might well hinder him in the search for work. The standard was not high. Some donors apparently believed that if the clothing was too good, it could be sold and the money used for other purposes. In this, as in other matters, the cynics had to be refuted. "Your committee," stated the 1927 report dryly, "are satisfied that clothing is converted into alcohol more in belief than practice."

The frustrations of this bleak period, when so much effort seemed to produce so little result, when problems seemed insoluble, statistics depressing, and support dwindling, were a little alleviated by the knowledge that the struggle was noted and the effort approved at the very highest level. King George V, who was patron of the Central Discharged Prisoners' Aid Society, in a message of encouragement sent to the local societies in 1927, stated that he had "always sympathised with the noble aims of the Society", and expressed his appreciation of the efforts of the voluntary workers.

5.   CHALLENGE AND CHANGE. 1935-82

Nearly three-quarters of a century had now passed since 1862, when the state had recognised the importance of the work of the Discharged Prisoners' Aid Societies by authorizing grants of money to them. Time had confirmed the official view that the after-care of prisoners was an essential part of penal practice, and there had been a consequent, if somewhat grudging increase in the financial aid, which now came from central, instead of local, funds. Some of the Societies, as we have seen, disbursed their money over-cautiously, and during the 1880s failure to claim the full amount of money available had resulted in a reduction of the total grant allocated to them.

However, during the next few decades the Prison Commissioners, taking greater interest in after-care, scrutinised the societies more closely and imposed new requirements which tended towards greater uniformity of procedure and organization. Meanwhile the grants continued, governed always by complex and varying formulae, which defined the relationship between local charitable giving and the number of prisoners discharged to the care of the local society. In 1923 an emergency grant was approved to help areas with special needs – among which Durham was included - and this was repeated in subsequent years until a more permanent arrangement was devised.

The standard of care regarded as acceptable, the complexity of the administration required to deal with different categories of prisoners, and the numbers of prisoners seeking aid were now increasing so greatly, that the discrepancy between the resources of the voluntary societies, in terms of money and skill, and the work which needed to be done, became increasingly evident. It became clear that a fundamental reappraisal of the whole subject could not be long delayed.

In 1932, a Departmental Committee, with Major Isidore Salmon as Chairman appointed, to review the methods of employing prisoners and helping them to find work on discharge, was extended to cover the methods and organization of the Aid Societies. Reporting in 1935, it concluded that the voluntary principle should be maintained to the fullest possible extent in after-care work, although "the policy of official co-operation and of Government contributions should undoubtedly continue." The work was one "for which the sympathy and active interest of the whole community need to be enlisted, and that, we are convinced, can best be done through an efficient voluntary organisation."[38] However, the

---

[38] Report of the Departmental Committee. Part II. Employment on discharge. Cmd. 4897.1935

Committee's recommendation of a new National Council to coordinate the work of the societies, in which the government agencies would be more closely involved, was rejected by the societies, with some ill-feeling, as likely to lead to a high degree of state control. The Societies then appointed their own committee of enquiry, chaired by Mr Francis P. Whitbread, whose proposals for a degree of reorganization and for strengthening the central body proved to be acceptable to both the Home Office and the societies. As a result, the Central Discharged Prisoners' Aid Society, which had existed since 1918, was reconstituted as the National Association of Discharged Prisoners' Aid Societies (NADPAS) in 1936. The Durham Society, along with most of the other societies became affiliated to this body, which from now on assisted the Home Office in assessing the worthiness of the societies to be awarded the statutory Certificate of Efficiency which entitled them to receive grants. To satisfy the new conditions, the Durham Society revised its rules in 1937, accepting the obligations, as required by the Prison Commissioners, to receive and apply Exchequer grants, to collect funds, to keep a record of their dealings with discharged prisoners, to publish an annual report, and to hold committee or sub-committee meetings not less than four times a year.

The new arrangement undoubtedly strengthened the Society, but the outbreak of war in 1939 brought dislocation and disturbance. Things were not made easier by the resignation of James Lister in the same year, following the death in 1937 of his wife, who was sorely missed. This ended the long period – nearly forty years – of exceptional stability, during which the work of Agent had been carried on by members of the family of Thomas Holmes. The Governor, Major Grew, gave generous help in this crisis, and assisted in the training of Joseph Brown, the new Agent, who, however, did not remain long with the Society, for he went off to active service in 1942, and was reported missing a year later. His place was taken by Mr F. Atack, who agreed to serve as Agent for the duration of the war. Mrs E. Allison, a very active and reliable worker, had succeeded Mrs Lister, and served the Society faithfully until 1954. The old Refuge, 19, Old Elvet, in which meals had been occasionally given to discharged prisoners and their relatives even after the death of Mrs Lister, was now commandeered by the military authorities for billeting troops, and the Agents worked from the prison and their own homes.

At the beginning of the war, one hundred and eighty-seven people were discharged from prison under an emergency measure, but all these were assisted by official funds. Thereafter, the numbers sentenced to prison remained substantial, partly as a consequence, it was thought, of the enlargement of war industries which attracted the kind of migrant worker who was liable to fall foul of the law. Wartime conditions brought new temptations for the women which many of them found impossible to resist, and the number of females in Durham prison had, by 1942, more than trebled. The increase in the work of the female Agent was acknowledged by an increase in her salary, which was raised to £80, with an additional £20 supplement.

The Society, indeed, was year by year devoting a larger proportion of its income to advising and counselling the ex-prisoners, through its Agents, and a smaller proportion to giving food and cash grants. This was the subject of a main comment in the annual report for 1951, over the signatures of Dean Alington, as Chairman, and Mr P.Q.H.Simon, the Secretary. They observed that the key to the Society's success or failure lay in the Agents' knowledge of the difficulties of the least fortunate part of society, partly in their ability to win the friendship and confidence of their clients and partly in a keen discernment and understanding of their characters. The Society, then, must be prepared to pay higher salaries, and this would be the most judicious and effective way of spending money. All the Societies experienced a fall in income during the war years, the result, no doubt, of a switch of public interest to war charities. Representations to the Home Office about the difficulties of carrying on without additional aid elicited an extra grant amounting to one third of the salaries of the Agents.

In the post-war world, the depth and intensity of the Society's problems increased. It was quite clear that the old ways of doing things would not at all adequately meet the needs of mid-twentieth century prisons. The nineteenth century machinery, which had barely coped with the rudimentary notions of after-care in the beginning, had been adapted a little and patched a little and required to conform to certain patterns, but it would need radical modernization if the Society was to make a significant contribution in the second half of the twentieth century.

Resources fell far short of what was needed, and the appeals for financial support bore an air of increasing desperation. The 1951 report, referring to a shortfall of £300, indicated that the Society would not be able to continue to function unless new sources of income could be found. Temporary easement came with the receipt of five years arrears of Bishop Wood's charity, but in 1953 income again failed to meet expenditure, though a contribution from the local authorities of £70 helped to lessen the gap. In that year the recommendations of the Committee on Discharged Prisoners' Aid Societies (known as the Maxwell Committee) that the government grant should cover half the approved administrative costs of societies and half of the expenditure on clothing, and that the payment of sums to meet the immediate subsistence needs of discharged prisoners would no longer be the responsibility of the societies, were greeted therefore with great relief.[39]

The other main recommendation of the Maxwell Report, that the local societies' sphere of responsibility should be limited to after-care in a literal sense and therefore should be exercised only after discharge and outside the prisons, while a new 'Prison Welfare Officer' should be appointed and controlled by NADPAS for the work inside the prisons, was, perhaps naturally, less well received. Yet some such development was inevitable in the long process which began when the government first accepted that there was an obligation on the imprisoning authority to take some thought for the prisoner's welfare on his release. For a long time, the burden of after-care had rested almost entirely on the voluntary societies, and the scale of assistance had been too low to allow significant help to be given where the need was greatest. With the acceptance of the principle that a higher standard of help was not only justifiable, but also morally imperative and economically beneficial, the costs of after-care soared to a point far beyond the resources of the voluntary sector, and state aid became more substantial. As the proportion of public money in the total spending increased, the authorities naturally insisted on a greater control over the procedures and policies of the societies. Now, the societies were compelled to surrender not only their autonomy, but also a share of the work. Yet there remained, and would remain, things to be done in the field of after-care which would be carried out by voluntary effort or not at all.

In the north-east, the Maxwell Report was the prelude to reorganization. Societies were being encouraged by the Home Office to reconsider and rationalise their geographical areas, and the North Riding Society, finding itself unable to cope with the rapidity of change and the ever-growing demands, had made an urgent request to Durham to take over responsibility for work in the North Riding. This was done on January 1st, 1954. With the work came the balance of the North Riding Society's funds, amounting to £155, and, more importantly, most of its subscribers, a number of whom continued to support the amalgamated body for many years. A new constitution incorporating the recommendations of the Maxwell Committee was devised, and came into force on January 1st, 1955, for the newly constituted County of Durham and North Riding Discharged Prisoners' Aid Society. The committees of the Durham Society and the Newcastle and

---

[39] Report of the Committee on Discharged Prisoners' Aid Societies. Cmd. 8879. 1953

Northumberland Society had also begun to work out a scheme for amalgamation during 1953, but this proved to be a false start, the Newcastle and Northumberland Society drawing back in 1954 after the approval of the Prison Commissioners had been secured. It was not until 1964 that this merger took place, with the encouragement of NADPAS, and the North Eastern Prison After Care Society was formed, with two regional committees based on Durham and Newcastle. Sir James Duff, formerly Vice-Chancellor of the University of Durham, was the first President and the Bishops of Durham and Newcastle were Vice-Presidents.

Even within the geographical bounds of Durham, the Society had from the start found great difficulty in establishing effective and harmonious relationships between the central committee and the scattered individuals and groups who offered aid to discharged prisoners in their own vicinities. Numerous efforts were made over the years to establish sub-committees or branches in the big centres of population. A particularly determined decentralising policy in the years 1928 and 1929 had resulted in the founding of branches in Middlesbrough, Darlington, Stanley and other towns. Some of them failed to survive for long, others maintained a more or less independent existence, but some worked actively and in fruitful relationship with the parent body. Two firmly based and well-supported branches carried on the work in Darlington and West Hartlepool for many years, raising money, and offering moral and practical support, in a variety of forms to returning ex-prisoners. Clothing or cash might be provided, accommodation found, employment sought, property redeemed, or company given on a court appearance. If desired, the homes and families of a man in prison were visited. In some cases long term contact was maintained, and ex-prisoners returned to the offices a number of times, sometimes over many years. Mr A. Brown, Chairman of the West Hartlepool Branch Committee in 1956, expressed their philosophy: "We do what we can always aiming that for every man on discharge the sentence just served shall be the last one."[40]

Throughout the area, the Society could still also refer to voluntary workers and Probation Officers working in sixteen towns, and it received constant practical help from such organizations as the Salvation Army, Toc H, the St Vincent de Paul Society, the W.V.S., Rotary, and many churches of a number of denominations.

From 1951, following a successful experimental arrangement at Wakefield (where the Manager of the local Employment Exchange was also a member of

---

[40] *Annual Report of the County of Durham and North Riding Discharged Prisoners' Aid Society for 1956*

the committee of the local Discharged Prisoners' Aid Society), Ministry of Labour Employment Exchanges adopted special procedures for placing discharged prisoners in jobs. While officers were reminded that "persons who have served terms of detention need particularly sympathetic treatment", they tried to "strike a proper balance between their responsibility to assist a discharged prisoner to obtain suitable employment and their responsibility to assist an employer to find a suitable worker for a vacancy." [41] In practice, they were very helpful in this traditionally most important of the responsibilities of the Discharged Prisoners' Aid Societies. Members of the Society and the Welfare Officers continued also to make special efforts in this field.

In accordance with the tenor of the Maxwell Committee's Report, the Durham Society continued to deploy most of its resources in the form of advice, and assistance in alleviating personal and family problems arising from, for example, the accumulation of debts, illness, loss of accommodation, estrangement between husband and wife, and, of course, unemployment. Fewer cash payments were necessary, since subsistence allowances were obtainable through the National Assistance Board, and the funds of the Society were devoted largely to the payment of salaries to the Welfare Officers who carried out these practical services, as well as to their travelling and administrative expenses. At this critical time for the aid societies, Durham was served well by its Welfare Officers. Mr Thomas McNamara, appointed in 1947 when he moved into 19, Old Elvet, had had extensive experience in voluntary social work with the St Vincent de Paul Society, and at once applied himself to the Society's work with great zeal and skill. Mrs Vesta Errington succeeded Mrs Allison in 1954. Brought up in the Salvation Army, she too was well equipped by experience and temperament for the work, to which she brought a very shrewd knowledge of human nature and a down-to-earth efficiency, enriched by qualities of humour, understanding and perseverance. She was convinced that it was not enough to get a man a job if the home circumstances were not right, and she tried where possible to establish a stable background for the discharged prisoner, acting in the belief that "if the home's right all else follows". Mr McNamara and Mrs Errington were now paying more visits, writing more letters and making more phone calls than ever before. On behalf of the ex-prisoners and their families, they interviewed landlords and landladies, interceded with Assistance Board officials and local authorities, reproached hostile neighbours, stopped evictions, found furniture, investigated unjustified claims, sought legal advice, reinforced inadequate personalities and distributed the occasional gifts received from charitable benefactors.

---

[41] *Memorandum submitted in evidence by the Ministry of Labour and National Service on the employment of discharged prisoners, in Report of the Committee on Discharged Prisoners' Aid Societies.*

In 1960, when Mr Joe Nixon, an ex-policeman, was appointed as the first of the Prison Welfare Officers envisaged in the Maxwell Report to work in Durham Prison, Mr McNamara and Mrs Errington became After Care Officers, and intensified their efforts in the field outside the prison.

The Durham Society had the good fortune to have the leadership of Dr G.H.Christie, Senior Lecturer in Chemistry in the University of Durham, as Chairman from 1953 until his death in 1965. His devotion to the ideals of the Society and his great administrative ability were recognised at national level by his election in 1955 as a member of the Executive Committee, and later as Vice-Chairman of the National Association of Discharged Prisoners' Aid Societies. Under his guidance the Durham Society was kept in touch with official thinking, and helped to understand the principles behind policy changes and the need to adapt its own ways to the modern world, even if this meant breaking away from the traditional moulds and adopting new postures. Not all of the local societies, however, proved willing to act in the spirit of the Maxwell Report, and its implementation was very uneven. The facts that very few of the local societies were financially strong enough to find even half the amount needed to pay salaries on the scale considered appropriate for their Welfare Officers (the other half being paid by the Home Office); that in a number of cases strong tensions were set up as a result of the juxtaposition of two sets of social workers doing similar work, the one inside, and the other outside, the prison, but with different employers and with very disparate employment conditions; that some of the societies were resolutely dilatory about responding to the suggestions of the Maxwell Report, continuing, for example, to operate the outmoded case committees; and that there was a fair amount of criticism of the societies at this time in the Home Office, the Prison Commission and among the general public, made it nearly inevitable that the changes consequential on the Maxwell Report would turn out to be only interim measures, and that further reorganization would follow.

When, in 1961, the Home Secretary asked the Advisory Council on the Treatment of Offenders (ACTO) to consider and report on the future organisation of prison after-care, it was by no means clear that the Discharged Prisoners' Aid Societies would survive in recognizable form. NADPAS, having adopted a new constitution, and recognising the weakness of a position which had given it no powers to coerce its recalcitrant member societies, addressed itself to preparing a realistic and flexible defence. A small but able sub-committee, consisting of Lady Inskip, Mr Staughton, and Dr Christie (Durham), was appointed to prepare evidence to be offered to ACTO. It accepted the need for substantial and imaginative reform if the demise of the voluntary societies was to be avoided, and recommended radical changes, which would have embodied a strong central voluntary, but state-funded, society, with powers to appoint and employ all the social after-care workers both inside and outside the prisons, and to control the work of the branches through the inspectorate.

While the ACTO Report was awaited with considerable apprehension, the Durham Society revised its own procedures in accordance with current practice, and discontinued the case committees which had been so strongly criticised. It was left to the Prison Welfare Officer, appointed, as we have seen, in 1960, to assess the needs of prisoners about to be discharged; but the Committee, anxious to do what it could in its part of the field, looked for volunteer associates in all parts of its area, who would be willing to reinforce the operations of the after-care officers by affording friendship, advice and support to ex-prisoners returning to their districts.

When it came, the Report confirmed the fears that formal after-care of prisoners would be very largely taken over by the state. It was to become the responsibility of the renamed Probation and After-Care Service. Under the discerning leadership of Dr Christie, the Durham Society accepted, though with some sadness, the loss of the status and functions which had characterised such societies for just over one hundred years (though the Durham Society had not been formed until twenty years after the 1862 Act). Disappointed though he was, Dr Christie accepted that resistance to the change would neither be justified nor successful, but he kept a steady course and remained confident in the future of the Society, never doubting that there would be work for it to do. "There will be ways," he said, "...by which State aid will be usefully supplemented and reinforced by voluntary charitable bodies such as ours."[42] Tragically, he died suddenly in 1965, but the society was now resolved to follow "in the direction to which he pointed", [43] and so began to search for other ways, which they knew must exist, of supporting prisoners, ex-prisoners and their families.

Deeply affected by the double loss of their traditional role and their strong chairman, the Committee of the Society remained united and committed, and resolved under the energetic chairmanship of Mr Tom Madrell, J.P., to face the challenge of an unfamiliar future, without grants or after-care officers and with a new constitution and a new, yet to be defined role. An altogether new kind of

---

[42] Annual Report, 1963
[43] Annual Report, 1964-65

relationship between the statutory and the voluntary agencies had to be worked out, and new ways of assisting in the rehabilitation of offenders devised. It was not surprising that a number of Discharged Prisoners' Aid Societies refused, or proved unable, to accept the new dispensation and ceased to exist.

The traditional functions of the Society in respect of clothing, accommodation, employment and other needs, economic and personal, were now transferred together with the officers, Mr Hope (who had worked for the Newcastle Society before the amalgamation and, latterly, for the Newcastle Committee) and Mr McNamara, to the statutory After-Care Service, and, on January 1st 1966, the Society became a purely voluntary body, without official grants or duties. In so far as it still offered assistance in these traditional areas, it was normally by means of small cash grants applied for by the Probation and After Care Officers on behalf of the men and women for whom they were responsible. By applying its limited resources to cases where a special need, not qualifying for help from statutory funds, had been identified by Probation Officers in Northumberland, Durham, Teesside, and the North Riding, the Society continued to help individual prisoners and their families in a compassionate and constructive way, as it still does.

One area in which there was by general agreement, a great deal of room for voluntary effort, was the provision of hostels, homes, half-way houses and other forms of accommodation for those discharged prisoners who were homeless, jobless, aimless and possessed, perhaps, of other disqualifications for normal social living. There never had been, perhaps never would be, enough of such places. At any rate, the North Eastern Society began to think along these lines, exploring the possibility of establishing a hostel for women in 19 Old Elvet, while in Newcastle, at 226, Westmorland Road, Abraham House, a home for discharged men who were seeking to reform their ways, was opened in April 1965, through the agency of Councillor Bennie Abrahams, a member of the Society committee, and his wife, and run with the help of an advisory committee from the Society. In the event the Durham hostel did not materialize, and Abraham House ran into difficulties and was closed in April 1970. The society was, however, able to help in supporting a number of hostel projects run by various bodies, voluntary and statutory, within its geographical boundaries.

Another effective contribution was the purchase in 1974 of a six-berth caravan which, sited not without difficulty in a coastal resort, provided holiday accommodation for a sizeable number of families whose lives had been impoverished by the imprisonment of one of their members, and who found refreshment and comfort in a temporary respite from the pressures of their normal life. Members of the Probation and After Care Service oversaw the management of the caravan, and arranged bookings through the summer for their client families, while all the costs were borne by the Society.

In 1970, it was decided to open the office building at 19, Old Elvet, as a centre for the use of families and friends of prisoners making visits to the prison, but the numbers using it were small, and after two years of devoted but frustrating service on the part of volunteer helpers, the project was abandoned. Some years later, the idea was revived with the encouragement of members of the Probation Service and, after thorough investigation of similar projects operating elsewhere, study of the local situation, and consultation with the Prison authorities, the Society opened a new Visitors' Centre on July 27th, 1981. With the loyal and imaginative support of many volunteers from the city and district, this venture survived, and the house at 19, Old Elvet, once again offered some of the warmth and practical help for families affected by criminal behaviour, which were characteristic of it in the earlier days of the century.

In the first hundred years since its inception, the Society had experienced more, perhaps, of difficulty and disappointment, frustration and sense of failure, accusation and criticism, than of success, gratification and satisfaction. It was criticized, on the one hand, for not doing enough to help discharged prisoners, and, on the other, for trying to do anything at all for the 'criminal classes'. Through it all, its members were sustained by the persistent conviction of the importance of their work, and the patient acceptance that disappointment was inevitable, as well as by the occasional experience of success, of an ex-prisoner made good, of a letter of thanks for a donation from a grateful client, of help and support from the community. The persistent failure of the public to give substantial support, whether by way of monetary contributions or attendance at meetings, was one of the most discouraging aspects for people who were nevertheless assured that they were engaged in a great work. It was not only the nature of this work but also the unusual relationship between a voluntary movement and an official department which was bound to cause problems . From the 1930s the finger of official doubt, and sometimes disapproval, pointed at the societies, shook their confidence and created insecurity.

The falling of the blow in 1963, when the state, after it had for one hundred years looked to the aid societies to provide acceptable levels of assistance for discharged prisoners, finally took the whole field of after-care into its own hands, was inevitable, and indeed was an acceptance and confirmation of the pioneering efforts of the voluntary societies. Moreover, though for some Societies it proved death, for the rest it presented a necessary challenge, forcing them to push their thinking further and seek new insights. Unless they blazed new trails, they would expire. The Durham Society, though the exploration was lengthy, found new, much needed and very rewarding work in supporting the families of prisoners. As the next section will show, they became active in the development of Prison Visitors' Centres and other services for families and friends visiting prisoners. At the same time, they did not lose sight of the needs of the prisoners themselves, during their sentences and afterwards.

PART II

Building Bridges for Prisoners, their families and the community

1882-2007

Introduction

I remember vividly when as a Probation Officer I was seconded to work within Durham Prison, and I used to walk regularly past queues of waiting visitors standing outside the main gate of the prison. It did not matter whether it was rain or sun, hot or cold, it just did not seem right to see families struggling with young children, young mothers carrying babies, grandparents or friends having to stand there waiting to be processed through for a brief visit, no matter what the conditions were or how long it took.

How things have changed! Ruth Cranfield brings the history of NEPACS up to date with an account of the last twenty-five years of its work with prisoners and their families. She describes the first faltering steps to establish a visitors centre at Durham prison and how, gradually working with the Prison and Probation Services, NEPACS has established itself throughout the north-east. Its expertise and reputation has grown both regionally and nationally and as a result it has built on its experience to develop other services for children and young people as well as continuing to educate and promote issues concerning the rehabilitation of offenders.

None of this would have been possible without the dedication and enthusiasm of its large number of volunteers over the years, more recently its staff and throughout its Committee and officers of the society. The history of NEPACS has been one of voluntary endeavour and of a clear and steadfast belief in its values and purpose, but you will also realize as you read this, how at times the Society has been spurred on by the vision and leadership shown by a few individuals. Ruth has faithfully chronicled some of these but has omitted to mention the most important figure for NEPACS in the last twenty-five years, that of herself! It is her vision, of work with the families of prisoners that took NEPACS out of the doldrums of the 60s and 70s and set the course for NEPACS` growth in the last twenty years. It is her dedication, enthusiasm and sheer hard work which set the tone for those who have worked with her and which encouraged and inspired so many of us to join and try and do our bit. NEPACS would not be where it is now without her.

This history of the last twenty-five years in the life of NEPACS is a real testimony to the work of Ruth Cranfield and the love and respect she inspires.

Jim Black
Chairman

Note to Part II

This part was written 25 years after Part I.

It is motivated, not so much by concern with the growth and development of NEPACS, as by the interest of examining and recording the process of change in the treatment of families and friends visiting prisoners during this period. This process follows a well-established pattern, in which volunteers begin to provide a service which they feel is required by justice and humanity, and in time, the state, accepting the need, endorses and partially funds it. We were active in pioneering work, and most of the projects were new, and ground-breaking.

Important contributions came from Probation Officers, who through their work with prisoners knew about the conditions of visitors and that what was needed was effort which it would be far beyond their capacity to supply; from the prison governors, without whose understanding of the injustice and cooperation in improvements, nothing would have happened; and from the voluntary movement which shared awareness, capacity and energy. Motives were again mixed; they were largely humanitarian and philanthropy-led, but had a utilitarian element, in the awareness that a discharged prisoner with a family to return to had a much greater chance of successful resettlement. The work was always seen as contributing to the reduction of crime.

RC 2007

1. ANTECEDENTS AND BEGINNINGS 1982-1987

In 1982, at the beginning of its second century of service, NEPACS had passed through some twenty years of the doldrums, looking for the way ahead, for the right wind to catch….. They, along with the other Discharged Prisoners' Aid Societies,[44] had been thrust into crisis by the removal (1965) of their traditional role of aftercare providers to the prisons, which was transferred to the Probation Service (which for a time became the Probation and Aftercare Service). At this critical time the society was fortunate to have as Chairman Dr G. H. Christie, Senior Lecturer in Chemistry in Durham University. Very able administratively and skilled in leadership, he was strongly committed to the purpose and work of the society, which he had chaired since 1953. He kept closely in touch with the National Association of Discharged Prisoners' Aid Societies (NADPAS), of which he was an Executive Committee member, and, since 1955, Vice Chairman. Seeing the bigger picture, he accepted regretfully that the amount of government money being disbursed through the Discharged Prisoners' Aid societies was too large, and the consistency of its disbursement too unreliable, to justify resistance to the change, but he kept a steady course and remained confident in the future of the society, never doubting that there would be work for it to do. "There will be ways", he said, "…by which State aid will be usefully supplemented and reinforced by voluntary charitable bodies such as ours."[45] Tragically he died suddenly in 1964, but the society was now resolved to follow "in the direction to which he pointed,"[46] and so began to search for other ways, which they knew must exist, of supporting prisoners, ex-prisoners and their families.

In 1965 the change, after a transition period, had become effective. NADPAS was replaced by NACRO (National Association for the Care and Rehabilitation of Offenders), the Probation Service now administered government funds for aftercare, some of the old Discharged Prisoners' Aid Societies folded, but NEPACS continued to look for some other way of contributing in a field where it was well aware of high levels of need, neglect and unhappiness. There followed some fifteen years of seeking, with much frustration and some success.

---

[44] The Durham Discharged Prisoners' Aid Society, with the encouragement of the Home Office to rationalize and consolidate their territories, had amalgamated with the North Riding DPAS in 1954, and further amalgamated with the Newcastle and Northumbria Society in 1964. The fully amalgamated Society took the title the North Eastern Prison After Care Society (NEPACS), signalling the altered function of the new body.

[45] Annual Report 1963

[46] Annual Report 1964-65

The local senior officers of Probation were concerned that so little support was offered to prisoners' families while so much was demanded of them. They had recognized that NEPACS was a voluntary body with commitment to this group and potential to deliver a substantial service, while NEPACS believed that this was work which they wanted to do and which they could do. They welcomed the support of Probation in their search.

Thought was given to using our building, 19, Old Elvet, which had in its time served as a Refuge for females leaving the prison. Reviving its use as a hostel was an early idea, but instead it became first a Prisoners' Wives Club (1968) and then a Family Visiting Centre (1970). Both of these ventures, in spite of enthusiastic support from the "ladies", failed to attract enough users, and lasted only a few years.

Convinced that something on similar lines could be done, and having kept, on the whole, a steady nerve, NEPACS was ready by the end of the 70s, with the goodwill of Probation and the Governor, to embark on a more developed scheme to create a Visitors' Centre for Durham prison in 19, Old Elvet. Held up by industrial action in the prison, the opening was delayed until 1981. Then, with a team of some 30 to 45 volunteers recruited from the churches and charities of Durham, we embarked on a project which turned out to be a real step into the future. The new Centre was handicapped by the failure of a plan to integrate it into the prison visiting procedure, which meant that people spending time there were missing their turn in the queue which formed outside the old prison gate. Consequently, a very small minority of the visitors used the centre, but nonetheless this was a challenging, and immensely important, experience for us.

Despite fears of unpopularity, the neighbours were very helpful, enabling us to serve hot drinks for several weeks during the first winter when the water supply was frozen. At a loss for a system of passing on the key to the teams who succeeded each other day by day, seven days a week, we asked the Manager of the Royal County Hotel, drawing attention to the similarities and differences between his and our clients, whether he could help. He agreed, and for several years we collected the key daily from the hotel reception desk.

We were fortunate that Jim Black, at that time Senior Probation Officer in Durham Prison, became in 1982 a co-opted member of the committee. In him we had support from one who shared our vision of how we could serve prisoners' families, and who could contribute the necessary knowledge of practicalities. He encouraged us in arranging study sessions, and taught us a lot about the prison scene, before he moved on to a new job in 1985. We also forged links with others in the movement, hosting a lively meeting with three delegates from the Brixton Visitors' Centre, who were hoping to build some form of national association of visitors' centres.

So we were trained and informed, inducted into an unfamiliar world, built into a team and given insight into the prison and the needs of those so unwillingly involved in it. Most of all, the experience raised the trust of the prison, so that when they were preparing to open their fine new visitors' centre in conjunction with the newly built reception wing, they looked to NEPACS to manage it, and it gave us confidence to accept the invitation.

This was the early days for such centres.[47] The essential injustice in expecting innocent families to pay such a heavy price as they did in supporting their family member was, apart from a book (*Prisoners and their families*) written by P Morris in 1965, not yet acknowledged. Acknowledgement would bring a cost, the families were no one's responsibility. Probation did what they could in the context of the offender's support, but the subject remained largely uninvestigated. This was about to change. In 1983, a small book by Jill Matthews, *Forgotten Victims*, published by NACRO, laid out some of the stark facts. Five years later, the first conference on the subject of prisoners' families was held at Bristol Polytechnic with 80 participants. NEPACS, represented by the secretary, was there. There was a feeling of discovery, of solidarity, and of determination not to let go. Three main recommendations were made: "First, the Prison Department must be persuaded to introduce better facilities for keeping in touch; secondly, a network of properly funded support groups must be established across the country; and, thirdly, a national coordinating agency is needed for these support groups."[48]

Other conferences followed (NEPACS was also there), at annual intervals. They had the good will of the Prison Department, represented by Ian Dunbar, the Director of Inmate Administration. Speaking at the 1992 conference, he disagreed with

---

[47] *The first visitors' centre was opened at HMP Winson Green, Birmingham, in 1969 (though the Prison Service's Visitors' Centre Good Practice Guidelines (1988) attributes the origin of such centres to Brixton in 1972). Winson Green was visited by Mary Cartwright, Senior Probation Officer, and Ruth Cranfield, Secretary, NEPACS, in 1986, in preparation for opening the centre at HMP Durham. By 1995, only 28 of the 132 prisons in England and Wales had visitors' centres.*

[48] *Light, R. (ed) Prisoners' Families, Bristol, 1989*

one speaker's claim that the conferences were not carried through. He said, "My experience of these conferences is that they are. I do not think it fanciful to say that these conferences have informed policy. The changes in family ties over this period have been quite considerable".

Among much that these conferences achieved, one very significant development was the establishment, in 1990, of the Federation of Prisoners' Families Support Groups, of which NEPACS was a founding member, and on which (including under its new name Action for Prisoners' Families,) we have had committee representation most of the time.

On April 21st 1987 the new centre opened in 22 Old Elvet, Durham. In its first years, a time of induction, experience, meeting with many other people involved, and learning, we were well supported by Avril Price (Senior Probation Officer) and Melvyn Jones (Governor 4). We had recruited widely, and began with new teams, each with a team leader to take ultimate responsibility. The centre was now built into the structure of the prison visits procedure. The work was more complex and more responsible, but our established methods of working proved transferable and adaptable. We were all new to the reception desk work, where we registered arrivals, recorded the order in which they came (which freed visitors from the tyranny of the queue), and sent them up to the prison as requested by the officers working on visits there. We were glad to be entrusted with this work (at one point it was suggested that an auxiliary officer would work with us on this) and knew that it must be done meticulously. The centre had a liminal role, between the ordinary world and the prison. The desk was the first encounter with the prison for the visitor, and it was vitally important to reassure and welcome, especially the first time visitors, many of whom were deeply distressed and fearful. It was a job needing unobtrusive efficiency, unfailing accuracy, and great compassion.

For the rest, we started by using the old informal methods, greatly reliant on the reliability and resourcefulness of the volunteers, who brought the house to life by opening the door on their rota day, until they locked up again and left it in peace. Teams were augmented from time to time by family members. There was no financial 'arrangement' with the prison, and the society was not wealthy. We had to charge for refreshments which were bought on an ad hoc basis from a local cash-and-carry, but kept the prices as low as we could. The daily diary became a kind of robust command centre, conveying administrative information, urgent needs and vigorous exhortations. The Newsletter was inaugurated as a calmer vehicle for the interchange of information and ideas. We were still improvising and operated very much in the spirit of "Keep calm and carry on!"[49]

The prison worked with us with great amiability, but can't have found it easy. While we delivered our duties efficiently, the normal lines of communication were absent and the situation precarious. The rota was composed for the year, and after that rota management was largely a matter for the team leaders. Stationery and stores were purchased when and how we could.

In 1986 NEPACS had embarked on work in another area, which would lead to substantial development. We opened a play project with a group of volunteers in the visits room in the new high security prison in Durham, HMP Frankland. This was one of the first such projects for children in prison. Looking back, it is incredible to think how long such provision for children was in coming, and how grim and forbidding an experience visiting their parent in prison must have been for children without it. This was the reason why so many parents wanted to leave their children with us in the early visitors' centre, and why we were willing to look after them.

A caravan project, which, after one or two hiccoughs, had been begun in 1975 with the encouragement of Peter Warburton, at that stage Assistant Chief Probation Officer in Durham, had been making a very effective contribution, year by year.[50]

During this testing period, the society continued to make cash grants in support of Probation Service clients and projects, in ever increasing amounts. Martin Jones, Assistant Chief Probation Officer, Durham, wrote about their value in the 1979 Annual Report, indicating how these funds were available when statutory agencies could not help. He mentioned, in particular, the contributions which made it possible for a short term prisoner to retain his accommodation while he served the sentence and so avoid becoming homeless, and the provision of small funds to support a constructive hobby for a prisoner. He mentioned also

---

[49] Notes in the diary hint at the blithe resourcefulness of the operation:
"Please note if fire alarm starts whistling, it means the water heating in kitchen is at fault"
"desk rather dangerous, nails exposed"
"change v. difficult as there was only 20p in coppers in the box"
"Does somebody know the needs of the palm?"
"Help! New boiler needed urgently"
"light bulb melted into shade in crèche – no answer from works department"
[50] See p.85f.

NEPACS financial support of the Darlington Lodgings Scheme which did useful work in providing lodgings for discharged prisoners, and a small annual subscription which enabled Probation Officers working in Low Newton and Durham to meet the special needs of women prisoners.

By 1987, then, the society had a new map. It had identified, in visitors' centres, children's projects and the caravan, new ways of working with prisoners, ex-prisoners and their families in areas which cried out for development. The next two decades saw the deepening and extension of this work in the North East of England. Alongside this activity, the old, basic function of making grants continued, sometimes feeding into and enriching the new projects, sometimes working independently to plug a hole or lend support to groups or individuals excluded from the benefits of the major activities.

19 Old Elvet:
the kitchen/reception room.

2. Moving Forward: the Visitors' Centres 1987-2007

These were 20 years of hard work and growth, of building relationships, becoming an employer and increasing the work-force, of developing employment policies and financial skills, recruiting, adopting new fund-raising and publicity strategies, of building the committee, developing the structures, working out new roles, and, above all, building up the provision of services for families of prisoners in the North East.

Roger Statham, Chief Probation Officer of Cleveland, was Chairman of NEPACS (1988-94) through this first critical juncture. He had the vision, the enthusiasm, the experience and creative skills which were needed. Despite his own heavy responsibilities, he found the time which NEPACS so much needed. The committee was still small and functioned through its quarterly meeting; and there was no Executive Committee. Roger's meetings with the secretary became dynamic sources of plans, proposals and ideas which propelled the society forward. He helped us to develop essential tools and practices. The committee was strengthened and became more active. Roger stressed that, in a time of economic stringency, finance was becoming an increasingly critical aspect of the society's work, and that we would need to put more and more energy into fund raising. A fund-raising sub-committee was formed, led by John Ayton.[51] Our grants, which were central to our work, were brought under the discipline of a policy (1993), which was not so arbitrary as to exclude the exercise of a wide discretion. A publicity sub-committee was also set up, which, among other things, began to publish a bi-annual Bulletin. A recruitment drive brought in a number of supporters from Cleveland, and some members and volunteers in Durham. A new logo and letterhead emerged from a competition in Teesside Polytechnic to build up our corporate image. Roger was much impressed by the commitment shown by the volunteers, and got to know many of them. He negotiated with the Home Office at a time when funds were extremely tight, and, with the support of Martin Mogg, Governor HMP Durham,[52] obtained a grant which allowed us to appoint a part-time coordinator of the Visitors' Centre in 1991. As part of his case, he urged that the partnership between the society and Durham Prison was an example of the best community links between the voluntary and statutory sectors. With this, and the enlargement of the grant in 1992 to make the post full-time, NEPACS took the first steps in development which led years later to the

---

[51] See further p.69f.

[52] He wrote to the Home Office, "There is no doubt that this facility considerably reduced the workload that would normally fall to prison officers and obviously makes the lot of families visiting more comfortable".

appointment of our Chief Executive Officer in 2008. When his six-year period in the Chair came to an end in 1994, we were extremely sorry, but knew that he left the society more fit and more confident than before.

Joanne Woods, a volunteer since 1987, was the first coordinator. She did an inspired job in helping us to cross over from our voluntary informality to a more disciplined, professional project, until the post became full-time. To cope with the immediate needs of employership a Personnel Sub-Committee was formed, which, expanded and adapted as need arose, developed employment policies and contracts of employment, carried out supervision and appraisal procedures, worked hard and served us well for the rest of this period.

It wasn't long before the pressure on space was felt in 22, Old Elvet, which was never really large enough for the numbers using it. Already in 1989, it was crowded, and in 1995 when the Inspector of Prisons reported favourably on the centre's services, reference was made to shortage of space and the inadequacy of the building. A number of proposals and plans about expanding the centre into the adjoining building have been made – twice the shared wall has been breached - but variation in the floor levels between the two houses has frustrated progress. Other proposals were made, but in the end the claims of the prison to space had higher priority. The situation remains very much the same 15 years later (we have lost a useful patio and gained a "conservatory" playroom).

These years were marked by growing difficulty. Poverty continued to dog much of the population, and the unemployment rate continued to rise, being higher in the North East than in the rest of the country. The prison population was going up year by year, not so much because crime was growing, as that sentences were heavier, longer. There was discontent among the prisoners which came to a head in the riots of 1990 in Strangeways and other prisons[53] which were followed by an enquiry led by Lord Justice Woolf resulting in the Woolf Report of 1991. The report put the view that, though they would not have expressed it in these terms, the prisoners felt a lack of justice in the prisons.[54] The concept of prisons having closer links with communities, which emerged ("that the walls

---

[53] We received an endorsement of the importance of visits in the prison system. The volunteer in the play area in Frankland, talking with the Governor, Al Papps, during the riots, commented that the atmosphere in the prison seemed good. "Yes", replied the Governor, "it is good. And I will keep my visits going, and it will remain good".

[54] John Howard from Durham Probation Service reminded us in his contribution to the Annual Report (1991) of Woolf's belief that prisons should be founded on the twin pillars of Security and Justice.

of the institution be made more permeable than in the past"),[55] interested NEPACS, since the concept of bridging the gap between prisons and the community is a very important part of our philosophy and our history. The rising profile of the visitors and the recognition that better arrangements for meeting their needs were urgently needed was reinforced by the Woolf Report. Among the findings, there was a recognition of the essential good service which the visitors gave to the prison, and among its recommendations for many liberal improvements in prison practice were a number of suggestions about improving conditions for visitors. The government accepted Woolf's key principles, and began to translate some of them into practice very soon (for example the times allotted to visits were made more generous and more flexible). The report was welcomed as the most progressive programme for prisons of the 20th century, and, as its implementation began, we saw signs of a new golden age for visitors.

It didn't last long. The publication in 1993 of Home Secretary Michael Howard's view that imprisonment should be a more austere experience and that "prison works" was followed in September 1994 and January 1995 by escapes from Whitemoor Special Security Unit and Parkhurst Prison respectively. These gave rise to the Woodcock and Learmont Reports, which triggered a massive reorientation towards security in prisons, believed by Judge Tumim to embody "the over-emphasis on security at the expense of humanity". Visitors, who seemed to revert to being primarily regarded as a security risk, found the consequences heavy, though some of the benefits flowing from Woolf did remain.

Security, which was not only concerned with attempts to assist escapes and the smuggling of weapons but also attempts to introduce drugs, dominated more and more the policy and attitude to visitors. The experience of visiting grew ever more formidable, as new and more intense search procedures - increasingly demanding proof of identity, drug dogs, photography, x-rays - and new rules about arrangement of furniture and regulation of behaviour were formulated. New Child Protection policies led to stricter regulations regarding children visiting. All of this, of course, made visits more forbidding for adults and for children, and it increased the likelihood of the visit being refused at the point of admission. The number of distressed and disappointed visitors requiring support and comfort rose, and with it the importance of, and the stress on, visitors' centre workers. Apart from the disappointment and vast inconvenience of such an upset visit, was the cost of the wasted journey. Where the visitors

---

[55] *Rod Morgan, in Prisoners' families: keeping in touch, by Roy Light 1992*

have spent all their spare cash in travelling to make the aborted visit, this is a considerable disaster.[56]

The need for visitors' centres was greater then ever. They had multiplied only slowly: by 1995 only 28 of the 132 prisons in England and Wales had a visitors' centre. The Prison Service now acknowledged their importance and required each new prison to be provided with a centre. It's true that views of the main function of a centre varied: for some, priority went to the support of visitors, while for others, particularly after 1995, the main function was to serve security. The Prison Service was ambivalent. With one voice, it followed the thinking of the Woolf Report, and in consultation with voluntary societies, led by The Federation of Prisoners' Families Support Groups, joined in publishing Guidelines for Visitors' Centres. In these works, the centre is there for the families, and this is the view of NEPACS. The origin of our centres lay partly in the need, while fully respecting the prison's authority and rules, to support and speak for a group of people who had no one else to speak for them. This would be the view of most of the prisons we work with.[57] However, this does not remove the subtle pressure which can be felt from prison personnel to become part of their service, to view the visitors primarily with the eyes of suspicion. We do need to be very clear about our role, while we work as colleagues with the prison.

The need for advocacy is high-lighted for us in an issue which has marked the current decade. As the numbers of prisoners kept rising inexorably,[58] the number of visits to the prisons, not only did not increase to match the population rise, but actually fell. This happened throughout the country, and certainly in the north-east.

---

[56] *As the numbers in prison continue to grow, the Prison Service has difficulty in housing new admissions, who may be held in transit as a place is sought, and for whom no location is recorded. Sometimes visitors arrive hoping to see, or, if not see, get news of their relative, who turns out not to be in the prison and of whom there is no record. We can make efforts to find the 'lost' one, and to give reassurance, in what could otherwise be a huge crisis for the family.*
[57] *It is endorsed in the* Statement of Purpose *drawn up by the Visitors' Centres Consultative Group convened by the Prison Service. "Visitors' Centres exist to meet the needs of adults and children visiting relatives or friends in prison. They aim to offer a safe, pleasant environment where all visitors are met with dignity and respect, provided with the facilities they need, and offered information, support and the opportunity to discuss the difficulties they may feel in confidence" (cited in the Visitors' Centre Good Practice Guidelines 1998)*
[58] *Some figures illustrate this: 1996 55,281; 1997 61,114; 1998 65,298; 1999 64,770.*

(Left) **22 Old Elvet;** *child playing, early years*

(Right) **Families on the way to prison**

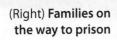

Numbers of visitors at north-eastern prisons 1992-2007

	98/99	99/00	00/01	01/02	02/03	03/04	04/05	05/06	06/07
Acklington	28,228		24,909	25,851	23,881	27,854	28,094	27,243	24,417
Durham	45,159		38,714	33.327	30,240	29,072	28,964	29,174	34,517
Frankland					14,543	13,785	14,233	13,785	14,505
Low Newton	16,574		10,011	10,202	10,313	9,180	8,887	10,583	9,449

Making allowance for the rise and fall of beds in a particular prison, the unreliability of the figures for Acklington/Castington, where the two establishments use one centre, and a clear distinction was not made between the two in the earlier years, and the changed role of Low Newton, the trend is clearly and markedly down. At a time when

    i. the importance of visits in the prison's day, and their contribution to the morale of the prison are accepted, and

    ii. the positive significance of the maintenance of family links for the success of rehabilitation and, in particular, the decline of reoffending is acknowledged,

this is an extremely worrying trend.

Even though phone-lines provide another means of maintaining contact, the diminution in visits is still very marked. Factors apparently deterring family and friends from visiting are clear to see: the difficulty in accessing telephone booking-lines, the increasingly heavy security procedures, the holding of more prisoners at greater distance from their friends and relations, and the expense of travel, the experience of being turned away from a visit which has been made in good faith and has cost precious money to make – all these in addition to the normal, considerable stress of visits. It is something which NEPACS tries to keep before the regional NOMS, and, through Action for Prisoners' Families, the national Prison Service.

Our work was never contained within the walls of the visitors' centres. Obviously the visitors brought their worries with them and sometimes wanted to talk about them. But in the absence of any support network outside (the wives' groups which had sometimes been supported by Probation had vanished) some family members rang us with their worries – often all they wanted was someone to whom they could talk about their concerns, who could understand and ease the isolation. We did manage the north-eastern office of the National Prisoners' Families Helpline from 2002 till 2005, but did not renew our bid when the number of branches was cut. We still are available on the telephone, and the evidence is that there is a great need for personal support.

NEPACS had pioneered visitors' centres in the north-east. We had given a lot of thought to their purpose, values and methods. As other prisons in the region began to think of creating visitors' centres, and referred to NEPACS, the question arose of what part we should play in the region which we claimed to serve. At first, with our slender resources, and no system or concept of contracting with prisons, we felt that we could do no more than play an advisory role in relation to those preparing to set up centres. We printed a guide to the establishment of visitors' centres which was circulated round the prison estate in the region and beyond. We added further advice and support in relation to HMP Acklington and HMP & YOI Low Newton. We also attended and advised the steering committee which set up the Holme House centre. As our position became more established, we were able to accept renewed invitations, and the Society adopted management of the visitors' centres at Low Newton (1997) and Acklington with Castington (1998). Frankland and Deerbolt were late to start, but NEPACS established their visitors' centres in 2002 and 2007 respectively. Holme House centre had, on our advice, been set up under an independent charity, but talks have recently been held about a possible transfer to NEPACS management.

NEPACS was stressed by these new responsibilities, some relatively far-flung. But the Society was resolved that the values and standards now formulated should be applied in all the projects. The Volunteers' Handbook, revised in 1999 and circulated to all volunteers, set out the principles and working standards which governed all work done in NEPACS projects.[59]

When Roger, having reached the end of his Chairman's term, had resigned in 1994, John Howard, Assistant Chief Officer in Durham, succeeded him in March, but in September that year had to withdraw in response to Home Office Circular 6/1993 which prohibited Probation Officers from entering into relationships with voluntary bodies, which might lead to conflicts of interest. This drew a new line, and distanced us, after nearly ninety years of working together, from our established allies and colleagues.[60] It took some time to find a successor.

Meanwhile John Ayton, who had joined the Society in 1987 and had rapidly become Vice-Chair, with the proviso that he would not be available for the

---

[59] For the section on visitors' centres, see Appendix 3.

[60] The Probation members became 'liaison officers' and continued to attend NEPACS committee meetings in a consultative capacity.

Opening of Visitors' Centre at HMYOI Deerbolt, 2007, by Anne Owers, Chief Inspector of Prisons (right), with Jenny Mooney (left), Governor of Deerbolt and Jim Black (centre) Chair of NEPACS.

Photo by kind permission of Newsquest North East Ltd

Chair, now in this new crisis, valiantly led the Society from the Vice-Chairmanship until December 1995. At a time of straitened finances, John had taken an active lead in fund-raising, inspiring others to activity and setting a high standard. As well as making a number of appeals to grant-making charities, he repeatedly negotiated hire without charge of a gracious room at the Three Tuns Hotel for events such as flower-arranging, cookery demonstrations, concerts, and talks, which not only raised funds, but also attracted a different congregation from our normal activities, and served our publicity drive as well. He gave generously of time and effort, opened his own home for volunteers' parties and events and served us patiently until the autumn of 1995.

In 1995 June Diffey, another volunteer, was appointed to a part-time post of coordinator. June's years as coordinator were important to us. Her meticulous, caring leadership, and the mutually respectful and cooperative relationships established with the prison staff, set a high standard. She made a distinguished contribution to the Committee of the FPFSG/APF, and on the Prison Service Family Ties Consultative Group, and her input to national work for prisoners' families enhanced NEPACS's reputation, and advanced the cause of prisoners' families. She stayed with us until 2007.

The search for a Chairman led at last to Brian Alport, former Assistant Director of Northumbria Probation, who agreed to serve. With his probation experience and specialism of having organized Norcare, a charitable company providing social housing largely for offenders, he brought with him a lot of skill and understanding, and led us forward for the next ten years (December 1995-2005). In particular, he negotiated a programme of Service Level Agreements to cover all the services supplied by NEPACS to the prisons, giving a measure of financial stability – although of course we remained conscious of the vagaries of prison budgets. This framework, supported by Donald Mackay as Appeals Officer (1995), allowed us to take on new responsibilities, notably the additional visitors' centres, and to employ extra staff as necessary. Brian's negotiating skills were tested by the discussions with the WRVS about taking over the Tea Bars,[61] and endorsed by the success of the change. In this period, the number of NEPACS employees rose very rapidly, though most of these were part-time workers, some for very few hours.

Brian also steered us through all the discussions and decisions of a period associated with self-examination and planning for future needs. An Executive

---

[61] See p.82f.

Committee, meeting monthly, was established in 1996, to deal with urgent matters and work in support of the main Committee, which became the Management Committee. A Review Day in 1998 brought together a number of people broadly representing all groups in NEPACS, to think about past, present and future. This turned out to be a preliminary event to 1999's Consultation Day ("Taking Stock and Moving Forward"), steered by Fred Robinson, which produced two important groups: a Communications Committee[62] charged with developing internal and external communications, and a Structures Committee to examine our structures which were acknowledged to be unfit to sustain the greatly expanded activities and responsibilities which NEPACS had assumed. The outcome from the Structure Group's labours was the adoption by NEPACS of status as a charitable Limited Company in May 2001 and, ultimately, the appointment of a Chief Executive in 2008. We have thereby entered a new phase of our history, but throughout the adoption of these changes, great pains were taken to make it clear that the aims and objectives and ethos of the Society remain unaltered.[63] Likewise, our dependence on, and value for, the volunteers remain as great as before. They are integral to the quality of the work which we do, and a vital part of it.

When Brian retired in 2005, we had already recruited Jim Black, newly back from Cambridge where he had been Assistant Chief Probation Officer, and now retired early, to the Board. At the beginning of this period, he had guided and informed us, and set our standards high. It was a serendipitous meeting soon after his return to Durham, which secured him for NEPACS again. Before long, he was Vice-Chair, and, in due course (2005), succeeded Brian in the Chair. He was, again, the man for the hour. He took responsibility in a turbulent time, with "difficult decisions to be made, all in the context of a changing Criminal Justice System".[64] The tea-bars were still settling down, the governance and structure of NEPACS were under review, we were still aware of tensions arising from the changed balance between volunteers and paid workers, we needed to find new ways of working with the altered criminal system, and to carry new projects and enterprises as well. Gifts of a high order were needed. Jim fortunately had them. He welcomed the challenges, valued what we did and believed we could do more, he encouraged us to engage with NOMS and the Government Office for the North East, and to form closer relationships with the Prison and Probation

---

[62] See Appendix 2

[63] "...The one thing that remains constant is the determination to assist in the rehabilitation of offenders and support of their dependants." Brian Alport in NEPACS Annual Report 2001-2.

[64] NEPACS Annual Report, 2004-05

Services, as well as with voluntary bodies. He helped us to maintain and raise our profile, regionally and nationally. The Board was strengthened. Above all, he remains committed to NEPACS values and purposes, and he relates with people as individuals whether they are prison governors, officers, staff or volunteers or users of our projects.

In 2005, when Ruth Cranfield retired after 25 years as Secretary, there was no great competition for the job, but, happily, Trish McDonald, though extremely busy, took it on gladly. Trish had been with us as a volunteer from the beginning, and had joined the NEPACS Committee in 1990. Besides her experience of years of teaching in Durham and Low Newton Prisons, Trish brought much wisdom and many gifts. Deeply serious about the purposes and aims of NEPACS, and passionate about the value and importance of each individual, she contrives, at the same time, when the time is right, that events will be fun. Her generosity and hospitality are legendary, within and without the Society, and her literary and artistic gifts enrich our activities and publications.

During this time, NEPACS's financial operations had grown rapidly and largely. While at the start of the period, our finances had been looked after by an employee of the bank, the time came when the banks could no longer offer this service. Treasurers were not easy to find, but we were fortunate to secure, successively, two genial, very talented and qualified people to look after our finances, Peter Lucas (1995-2005) and Clive Constance (2005-). Both worked with us during a period of great expansion and change, both found the work more complicated and time-consuming than had been predicted, and neither complained. In 2003, with the advent of Tea Bar responsibility, involving increased volume and complexity of accounting and engagement with VAT, a part-time Finance Officer was appointed. He computerized the finance system, fitting it to cope with our developing needs.

A fund-raising committee had been, as we have seen, established in 1988. In 1995 we invited Donald Mackay, newly retiring from the post of Fund Raiser at Finchale Training College to join our Board as Honorary Appeals Officer. He did so, to our great benefit. He brought enormous enthusiasm to the office, and his assiduous programme of appeals has raised many thousands of pounds, for our charitable purposes. He further helped us with our social fund-raising events. Concerts, coffee mornings, conferences and functions did not take place, and would certainly not have gone so smoothly, without Donald's attaché-case, full of drawing pins, rulers, blutack, scissors, bags, and everything that could imaginably be needed. Many of the beneficiaries of NEPACS's activities and grants have good reason to thank him.

We have looked at the visitors' centres, which became the basis of so much of the work of this quarter century and considered the structural development of the Society. Many other things were happening, and we shall look at their development in separate sections always remembering that they were part of one organic process, founded upon the purposes of NEPACS. We shall consider;

The Children's Projects (including the Special Children's Visits)
The Young People's Projects
The Teabars
The Grants
The Awards scheme
The Conferences
The Communications group
The Volunteers

(Left) **Officer plays Santa for a Children's Project Christmas party**

(Right) **Special Visit Low Newton**

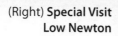

3. PROJECTS AND PURSUITS

The Children's Projects

In the early 1980s, children found prison visits rooms forbidding and unfriendly places. In the huge rooms, there was nowhere, other than their parents' visits table, to go, nothing to do. What an experience for the children! This is a main reason why so many children were left with us in the early days. The extension of the time allowed for visits just made things worse. The children were tired, bored, restless; they got on others' nerves: people shouted at them; they shouted back. All in all, the visit cannot always have done a great deal to foster family ties. Frankland was among the first prisons to have a children's play project, which was established by NEPACS in 1986. A few volunteers were collected together, they were addressed on security issues by a prison officer, and then took daily charge of quite a generous area, which we equipped with a variety of good quality toys and art materials. Apart from blutack, there wasn't much restriction on what we could have. Many toys were donated, including a loveable rocking-llama made for us in the prison workshop, which was very picturesque, but none too stable. Before long, we refurbished our equipment with the aid of a generous grant from BBC Children in Need. We were - and still are - determined that the nature and condition of the toys would reflect the high value in which we held the children.

Volunteer numbers were quite reasonable at first, and we could work in pairs, but the project suffered through distance from Durham, and the loneliness of volunteering – volunteers turned up for their shift, went into the prison, came out and went home, without any of the cheerful camaraderie of a visitors' centre to gather in. The group found leaders, and were brought together in occasional meetings, in the interests of consistency and togetherness. Members were very loyal, and pressure was somewhat relieved when we began to share volunteers (1991) with Durham. Still, in 1992, the group's leader sighed, "the overwhelming feeling was one of struggle". For nine years, the play area was carried on as a voluntary endeavour, until in 1995 a small annual payment was negotiated with the prison, which allowed the employment of a Play Facilitator to take responsibility for care of the materials and the rota as well as covering some sessions herself. The scheme was greatly invigorated by this small cash injection, the first acknowledgement by the prison of the value of this work.

At first, the children's play project had been viewed somewhat askance by the officers. They couldn't think why we did it, etc. "There go our future customers," they said. We didn't feel welcome. But they came round when they saw the difference in visits. "Where were you yesterday?" they then lamented about a day when there was no volunteer, "It was chaos!" The obvious appreciation of children, parents and (some) prison staff was always a great encouragement. The children's project makes a huge contribution in this high security prison, with prisoners serving many years and families characteristically travelling long distances. Families tend to visit in a regular pattern, so that staff and volunteers, who also work regularly, get to know the children, to expect them, and to form relationships. When children arrive, they find someone with whom they are familiar and toys which they know. It makes a significant contribution to a very long and tedious day. The sadness of seeing children arrive as infants, and reach school age and continue to visit and experience a relationship with their father, is tempered by the pleasure of witnessing the growing closeness, and the knowledge of our contribution to something so important.

NEPACS playworkers understand that their primary purpose is to support the bond between the child and the imprisoned parent. They do not see themselves or the toys as being the main business of the child, and continually encourage engagement with the parent. The children may take the pictures they have drawn and the toys to their family table.

Other NEPACS children's prison play projects followed: Durham (1990), Low Newton and Acklington (2000),[65] Deerbolt (2001), after a couple of aborted plans, and Castington (2005) after similar hesitation. Most recently, NEPACS has, at the invitation of the Prison, taken over the running of the play area in Holme House, (December 2005). We were always encouraged by the obvious appreciation of children and parents, and have treasured numerous acknowledgements.

"This is a good prison There's lots of place to play, lots of toys for everybody. In some prisons there is nowhere to play. In some they only let babies play and shoo away big children. I've been in a lot of prisons and this is a GOOD prison"
(an 8-year-old in Frankland, 1989)
"I like coming to play with the teachers, and I don't mind seeing my dad either"
(Durham)
"Do you have to pay to play in here"?
(wide-eyed) (Acklington)

In the Durham visitors' centre itself, from the beginning we had the children's room, though when considerations of safety caused us to bring this downstairs,

---

[65] The founding of the Play Project at Acklington was part-funded by Kids VIP

we were greatly constrained for space. There were perpetual conflicts of interest between children and adults, buggies and ankles, those coming in and those going out. At last money was raised by an appeal launched by Donald Mackay, which allowed us to erect, with some prison support, a very fine conservatory type annex on the back wall, which has served the children well since being opened in 1998. Projects for similar extensions have been mooted for other centres, which always have a dedicated space for the children, but which are invariably very short of room.

As we have seen, the early operations were for some time run very cheaply, and were financed from the society's own funds or visitors' centre grants, until 1995 when play workers were appointed in Frankland, and Durham. As the children's work expanded in complexity and amount, other play workers were appointed and it became necessary to appoint a coordinating manager to oversee the children's work in the region. The play projects are strongly supported by workers and volunteers, and have close links with APF and Kids VIP. They are involved with the APF's Family Friendly events, and other such initiatives. We were very excited when, in 2006, children from our projects were winners in each of the three age categories of the APF's Christmas Card Prize

Special Children's Visits

Inspired by the news of the All Day visits started in HMP Holloway in 1991 which were supported by the Save the Children Fund, we proposed that we should develop a similar project for children and their fathers in Durham Prison. With the support of the lively governor responsible for visits, the Chaplain, and one of the Senior Officers, Probation, our coordinator and some of our own volunteers, a series of meetings was held to plan the visits, which were clearly designated as being for the benefit of the children, and which began in 1993. Because the purpose of the visits was to support the child, it did not count as part of the father's entitlement to visits. A large grant of money from the BBC Children in Need Fund allowed the generous provision of toys and equipment, including material to allow active involvement of fathers in playing, with goals, tunnels, construction and craftwork materials, dolls, kitchens, etc. The Chaplain welcomed the involvement of the chapel, which, with the altar protected by a barrier of chairs, offered a generous, friendly space for both active and quiet play, and comfortable seats for those who just wanted to sit and talk to each other. The toys were stored in the choir loft when not in use.

NEPACS volunteers always attended the sessions. At first we thought we might have to support the fathers and facilitate their activities with their children.

It soon became clear that this would be, in the main, unnecessary. The men displayed the greatest ease and affection with their children, and the sessions were times of fun and understanding between parents and children. People who attended regularly, and those occasional visitors who came to observe because their own prison was considering the idea, found the contrast between the image of the prison, its harshness and macho culture, and the delicacy, order and spontaneous affection of the meeting between fathers and children deeply affecting and surprisingly beautiful. At first the uniformed presence was very discreet, but increasing stress on security made it more evident. The men were searched after the visit, and it was well understood that any engagement with illicit substances would stop the visits for the culprit, as well as imperil the whole project.

The children loved the visits, which went some way to providing the good quality contact with the parent to which the child is entitled (United Nations Convention on the Rights of the Child, Article 9). One child of 8 who was devoted to his father always saved his news to be given to his father at the visits. After the ordinary visit in the huge intimidating visits room, when the mother asked him, had he told his Dad, he would always look confused and say that he had forgotten. At the special visit, he simply sat with his father and they talked together all the time.

The wives/carers accompanied the children to the chapel to meet their fathers, and for a few minutes the family group was together. Then the wives/carers left children and dads together. At this time they could return to the visitors' centre to have coffee and talk together if they wished. It was a time of relaxing. Having handed over care of the children for a short time to their fathers they enjoyed the chance to chat – about problems of visiting, perhaps, or just day-to-day events, or the difficulties of managing on their own. Sometimes a Probation Officer came down to offer support and discuss concerns. It was a kind of wives' group, and some good relationships were formed.

In 1998 similar visits were introduced for women serving long sentences in H-Wing, Durham, and maintained until the wing was closed. Visits between children and their mothers in Low Newton began in 1999. These visits are of great importance and very precious for the mothers as well as the children, and the visits now take place at weekly intervals. In addition, "all-day visits", which involve a meal provided by the mothers, are arranged during the school holidays. Sometimes the carers spend the night before the visit in Durham. For children in care, who are seldom brought to the normal visits, it has been found that Social

Workers will make every effort to bring the children on the special visits, which they rate very highly. At these times the visitors' centre stays open all day to support the mothers and carers, and the whole arrangement is of the greatest benefit to, and is thoroughly enjoyed and valued by, all who take part.

Talks have been held for many years about the possibility of similar visits in Frankland and Acklington, but, so far, without positive result.

Young Peoples' Project

From the beginning of our work with prisoners' families, we were uneasily aware of the unmet needs of the older children. We tried hard to include them in our thinking and provision; thus we provided among the equipment more demanding jigsaws, puzzles and pictures, and had packs of cards in the cupboards. Occasionally it was possible to set up a table apart from the little ones' area, at which the teenagers could gather, or to adopt other ways of signalling that their presence was noted and desired. But it was difficult and we were aware of a neglected range of ages between young children and adults.

The news, in 2000, that the Federation of Prisoners' Families Support Groups had secured funding from the Diana Princess of Wales Memorial Fund for a three-year project to research the needs of this age group was tremendously exciting, especially when we heard that NEPACS would be involved in the development of the initial research project, and be one of the four agencies managing pilot projects in the 2nd and 3rd years.

One of the main problems for the researchers was the elusiveness, even the invisibility, of teenagers. Alienated by the difficulties of their lives in general, the increased sensitivity of their current situation, and their distrust of adult intervention, they tended to keep their heads down, and were most reluctant to be involved. But the north-east found an adequate number of young contacts, some of them from the NEPACS projects, for the research. The report based on the research contributed importantly to the understanding of the needs of young people with a parent in prison.[66]

In years 2 and 3 of the project, we employed, with funding from the Diana Trust, a youth worker, supervised by a group of NEPACS Trustees, to establish the youth project in Durham. An Activity Room was reserved for the young people, and

---

[66] *No-one's Ever Asked Me: Young People with a Prisoner in the Family*, by Kelli Brown, et al. 2001

equipped, with their involvement, with relevant and attractive games and material, including computers and electronic games, as well as table football and other activities for group play. Outreach work included home visits and escorting young people on visits, and community awareness-raising. Since that time, the Society, though unable to afford a full-time post, has employed a young people's worker and continued to make provision for the age group in the visitors' centre in Durham, and to campaign (so far fruitlessly, but with some Prison Service support) for a youth area to be provided in the prison visits room. In 2008, similar projects were established in Low Newton and Frankland, and we have ambitions to expand the work of the projects further, not only into the other north eastern prisons, but also into the community.

We have aimed to provide spaces where the young people have ownership, where they influence the decoration, the activities and the discipline of the room. We try to provide support in an unobtrusive and impartial manner, in a context where the activities are engaging and constructive to the users. The aim is to make the visit enjoyable, interesting and informative, and to facilitate contacts between the young people themselves, all of which, it is hoped, will increase their confidence in themselves and in their situation, and encourage communication and engagement with the imprisoned parent. There is a setting in which, and a person to whom, the youths can discuss their questions, uncertainties and fears. For many of these young people, silence about their situation is enjoined by their family or their context. At home they may be deeply isolated and lonely. They may experience long-lasting damage. Our youth projects provide support of an unusual and timely kind. It is much to be wished that similar facilities should be available at every prison, but, as far as we know, there is no similar provision for young people at other English prisons.

Tea Bars

Refreshments play a vital part in the prison visits room. They provide a focal point for the family gathering, and a suggestion of normality to the meeting. They allow the visitors an opportunity to express their love and support for the prisoner by providing food, and offer a civilized setting for other visitors. Since anyone could remember, this service had been provided by the WRVS. In 2002, as part of their retrenchment process, the WRVS nationally decided to withdraw from the prisons, leaving a huge gap. In the North East, NEPACS was invited to fill the gap. This was not something which we would have sought at this time, but we understood the importance of refreshments to visits, and that it would have been really sad to replace the human service by drink and chocolate dispensers.

The bullet was bitten, and enormously complicated negotiations entered into. The whole process reached completion in March 2003, when the running of the tea bars in seven prisons had been adopted. The whole activity of tea bar operation had been governed by a fairly ancient arrangement between the Prison Service and the WRVS, but each prison scheme was organized individually, and different arrangements were in place. In different prisons the teams had their own suppliers, and their own arrangements with the prison finance officer. We took the necessary step of appointing a Manager to integrate arrangements over the whole area, and a finance officer to pay the bills, manage the VAT arrangements and keep the accounts.

A number of the WRVS volunteers agreed to stay and work with NEPACS, but some tensions arose from clashing ideologies and different expectations. Some much valued WRVS volunteers are still with us, but there has been great and urgent need to recruit more volunteers in each location. The number of visits sessions has increased, and we have set ourselves the hard task of staffing every session. This was particularly challenging in the distant north and south of the area, and it became necessary to employ more staff. With the aid of volunteer bureaux and local populations, the manager, and the loyal staff and volunteers, some of whom work across the projects and prisons, the project is operating strongly. The tea bar workers are very busy, but they take time to be friendly and their support is much valued by the, often exhausted, people making the visits.

The work was always very demanding, involving high-pressure service for a relatively short time. When, in 2005, the Prison Service security teams began to ask that all drinks should be opened, decanted into polystyrene beakers, and covered with lids (the sugar, if required, having been added), the pressure increased, and other requests have added stress: e.g. the contents of food packages to be emptied on to a plate. All this was coped with, so great is the enthusiasm of staff and volunteers. Meanwhile efforts were and are made to introduce more healthy options where possible, and this has involved savoury foods, yogurts, cheese and fruit. While operating to a separate account, the operation, staff and volunteers of the Tea Bars are well integrated with the other projects and staff, thus giving and gaining strength to and from the whole.

. *"You are all great to do this for us you make us feel like normal customers coming for a cup of tea, not criminals".*
"Thank you for opening in the evening – it is nice to talk to a person and not a machine" (comment from Holme House)
"Thank you very much for your kindness while I have been visiting. It has been truly appreciated"

(Above) **Tea Bar:**
with Sandy Anderson, Tea Bar Manager

(Above) **NEPACS caravan and volunteer**

The Caravans Project

As part of the process of reassessment in the 1960s, NEPACS had in consultation with the Home Office, NACRO and Probation considered such projects as hostels of various kinds, and had finally decided to buy and maintain a caravan at the seaside, where weary families could have a holiday. With considerable effort the money was found to purchase the van, and a site at Crimdon Dene acquired. The caravan opened its doors in 1975. There was not, at this time, a lot of hands-on work from the Society. By 1982 Durham Probation Service (through the Peterlee Office) looked after most of the administration, while the equipment, repairs, etc, were funded by NEPACS. The Probation representative reported at Committee meetings on the progress of the scheme, and the projects sub-committee made occasional visits to the site. In 1983, there was talk of providing a second caravan, but it was felt better to look out for a larger replacement, and to improve the facilities. In 1984 an 8-berth caravan was purchased at a cost of £2,300, and it was connected with electricity and sewage services, provided with a TV and refrigerator, which very much improved the accommodation. The Projects Sub-committee undertook to keep in more regular touch by visiting the site and meeting those who administered the van. At this time a pleasant feature of the scheme – which was to be repeated at other places and times – was the friendship and voluntary assistance of a permanent neighbour on the site.

The re-siting at this time of our van on a site close to the railway line provoked anxiety on behalf of the many children who would occupy it, and involved members of the society in correspondence with the Council and British Rail. This led to the very necessary strengthening of the safety fence. In 1989, the on-site work with the caravan was transferred to the Hartlepool Probation Office, and thus to the Cleveland Service, and continued to flourish there, until 1994, when the whole project was moved to Cresswell in Northumbria, and the care of the Northumbria Probation Service.

This move severely strained the finances of the society, since the existing caravan had to be abandoned in Cleveland as the amenities and requirements at the new park were of a higher standard. But, by the same token, it much enhanced the quality of the holiday offered. Three years later, in 1997, the project faced another blow, with the news that Northumbria Probation Service could no longer justify the time spent in administering the project, and were forced to withdraw. Our great good fortune in this crisis was twofold. Firstly, Joan McArthur, who, as an employee of the Durham Probation Service, had looked after the booking since 1984, and when it was removed from her schedule of work had carried it on as a volunteer, was willing to continue, and is still with us. Her experience and goodwill has made a quite invaluable contribution to the welfare of the project. And secondly, Mark Kelly, the probation volunteer who had worked in the project, was willing to transfer his skills and interest to NEPACS, and, joined and supported by his wife, Eleanor, continues (in 2009) to give a wonderful service to everyone connected with the caravan, including the users, the society, and the site office. This is no mean assignment. Apart from the routine Wednesday visits to oversee the departures and arrivals, there are the alarms and disasters: fights on the site, a family running out of money half way through the holiday, the site staff making judgments (sometimes justified, sometimes not) about our tenants, travel problems . Mark and Eleanor seem to enjoy it all! They also look after a small number of volunteers. A second caravan was added to the project in 1996, and it has been a particular and successful interest of our Appeals Officer, Donald Mackay, to raise the funds for regular replacement and payment of the annual site-fees and expenses. The Caravan Sub-Committee works hard, keeps in touch with the site office, and makes regular site-visits.

An interesting feature of the scheme is the use of the caravans by families with a member serving a sentence in the near-by Acklington prison, who can book accumulated visits and so visit their family member in the pleasant context of a caravan holiday, instead of the usual long exhausting trek from a distant home. It is a very much appreciated facility. We received a long letter from visitors from Scotland:

"The Caravan is certainly a wonderful concept, and is a service which is designed to help the families of prisoners, families who like us are also innocent "victims", and hurting almost as much as the socially accepted victims of crime.
Could we suggest that NEPACS really stands for:
Non-judgmental, Empathetic, People,
Applying Compassion and Sympathy"

"The mother feels that NEPACS has enabled her family to function as it might if their father were not in custody"

"The caravan holidays and the grants made are highly significant in the lives of individuals."
Hana Knotek, Assistant Chief Officer, Northumbria Probation in
NEPACS Annual Report 2004-05

The Grants

From the very beginning, making grants from its limited resources has been a core activity of NEPACS. Its funds consisted of a number of historic charitable bequests given to aid poor prisoners, supplemented by current subscriptions and donations. These were subsidized from government grants in increasing amounts, until their 1960s reassignment to the Probation Service. Thereafter, NEPACS no longer employed welfare officers, but continued to support prisoners, ex-prisoners and their families by small grants, requested usually by the Probation Service.

Discharged prisoners still have a host of unmet needs, in the old areas of housing, employment and subsistence, sometimes taking new forms but always persistent. Families also have needs, in circumstances made harsher by the imprisonment. In the years 1982-2007, NEPACS grants increased in response to pressure of demand, and grew year by year, rising from £1318 in 1982 to £31,033 in 2006-07. Probation Officers found NEPACS a useful resource in their work, and again and again expressed this in their annual messages. Moreover they showed their appreciation in tangible ways, by raising money to support us: officers ran in Marathons for NEPACS, they held events in support, they attended our fund-raising efforts and passed on donations they received. Some joined the society.

Poverty and unemployment were increasing everywhere through the 1980s, the north east being particularly hard hit. State benefit was cut to the bone, and the numbers in prison rose. In 1988, changes in the DHSS system largely replaced the useful crisis grants with a system of loans, stipulating that loans should only be authorized when there was a real chance of their being repaid, which of course excluded the very poorest from access to them. Probation forecast that for their clients, NEPACS would often be the only resort other than the loan-sharks, into whose hands many would disastrously fall. Looking at a bleak future, Probation hoped that we would be able to increase our funds to meet the rising demand. Surprisingly, we did. In 1999 the Northumbria Divisional Director wrote, "I continue to be lost in admiration for the imagination and innovation displayed by NEPACS. In an era where resources are difficult to come by, somehow NEPACS manages not only to hold its own but to expand its operation to the benefit of the Probation Service, the people it supervises and their families – often the forgotten victims of the crime and criminal activity".

Since 1993, NEPACS grants have been governed by a grants policy, revised as necessary, but in essence focused on the rehabilitative needs of the offenders, accommodation, employment and clothing. Grants continued to be made flexibly (within the policy), imaginatively and promptly. Probation Officers welcomed our more flexible approach, which allowed grants to be made in unusual situations. They were encouraged by the speedy response, in situations which were often dire. The grants helped to reinforce the beneficent relationship with their 'clients', and we believed that this enhanced their value.

Accommodation grants occasionally meant a contribution towards a housing bond; or might pay for minimum furniture and equipment to make a new, empty, Council flat habitable, or provide essential reconditioned equipment (e.g. cooker, washing machine). They might pay for the relocation of a family threatened with violence, or a released prisoner not wanting to resettle among the criminal associates of the past, or the storage of a person's possessions to prevent their complete loss while a short sentence was served. In many situations, threatened and complete disaster can be averted by judicious use of a relatively small sum, which is simply beyond the applicant's means. It is usually the person who has none of the requisites of successful resettlement, for whose case NEPACS is the only resource. In these hard times, desperation is not far away. One application was for a small amount to pay for some bed and breakfast nights for a Cleveland lad who was currently living rough in the car park of a supermarket. In the event, the grant was acknowledged with gratitude, having been used instead to provide him with a tent and sleeping bag for use certainly in the car park, but which would make him more comfortable during the winter months. This was only a partial solution. Accommodation with an address is a prerequisite for any kind of restoration to society, and grants for this purpose are particularly important.

Employment grants assist another pathway to resettlement by helping to provide necessary equipment, clothing, training, qualifications, and so help in overcoming a multitude of hurdles in the way of getting a job. One grateful recipient from Teesside turned up at one of our visitors' centres, asking for the person whose name had been on the correspondence (which had become somewhat involved). He had called to say his thank-you; he had done the course, got the job, found a flat, got married and just had a little boy! A well satisfied client, who had taken the chance offered, had made good, and had no intention of offending again.

The grants for clothing cover a wide range of needs: it may be that they will provide clothing for job-seeking and interview, clothes appropriate for a new job, basic clothing to fill the place of clothes which have been disposed of by police, landlords, enemies or angry friends, clothing to keep its wearers warm or to give a destitute person a measure of self-esteem and confidence as he faces resettlement in a hostile world. It may be warm clothes for the family or school uniform to ease the transition to a big new school. Such grants make a real contribution to resettlement, whether by opening the way to work or giving the means of self-respect to someone who is otherwise spending his time in clothes belonging to his brother or his friends, or supporting the family.

Grants to serving prisoners are, in general, rarely available. NEPACS however regards them as important. While having a clearly humanitarian, charitable purpose, they can also be recognized to contribute to the resettlement programme, by providing for isolated prisoners a contact with the outside world and a message that they are not totally rejected by the society which they are likely to rejoin. NEPACS notably serves the families of prisoners in a number of ways, and through them their imprisoned relatives. By our grants to isolated prisoners, we go some very small way to redress the situation where those with families receive visits, correspondence, extra cash, while those without get none of these things,[67] and face a prospect of much higher probability of failure to make a successful resettlement.[68] The grants to serving prisoners are typically small. They may provide the means of purchasing hobby material or art materials or study books, which will help to make the sentence more tolerable and constructive, and the prisoner to have a more tranquil state of mind. They may even enable an isolated prisoner to preserve his self-esteem by buying small items of clothing. It may be that this privilege has been earned through the incentives scheme, but that the prisoner has no cash to buy the means of exercising his privilege. (Many of the earned privileges do rely on the families and friends of prisoners to finance them.) The issue is certainly vexed. Should NEPACS be relied on to provide levels of decency or care which the Prison Service do not? In principle, perhaps not. But, in practice, the answer is sometimes less clear: take, for example, the case of a young man suffering from asthma, whose prison nurse acknowledged that a special pillow, which the prison wouldn't provide, would make his nights more tolerable - NEPACS supplied the pillow at a very modest cost. Or, again, in Low Newton, for a young woman in the latest stages of pregnancy for whom no prison clothing was available, NEPACS made a small grant. It seems that such grants could be seen as supporting the legitimacy

---

[67] Some, it is true, receive visits or letters through the NAOPV, New Bridge, etc., but there are a great many who do not.
[68] 'The Home Office has also acknowledged that "Research…indicates that good family ties can reduce a prisoner's risk of re-offending by six times" '. Prison Factfile, March 2004, published by the Prison Reform Trust

of the prison regime, fostering a better relationship between the prisoner and the prison, and so reinforcing the rehabilitative purpose.

The grants, then, in this period, continued to be focused on the old rehabilitative needs. They were made flexibly, imaginatively, and promptly. We found that they encouraged the Probation Officers, and helped to reinforce the beneficient relationship with their 'clients', that they assisted the prisons in their duty to lead the prisoner towards living a good and useful life, and demonstrated that there was some goodwill for offenders and ex-offenders in the community. We believed that our grants were making a particular contribution to the reduction of reoffending and therefore of crime.

The Awards Scheme, 2004

Engaged as we were in our own projects, we recognized that NEPACS was well positioned to recognize and encourage imaginative and creative work with a rehabilitative purpose, by individuals in the prison and probation services, and, on Jim Black's suggestion, we resolved to establish an Annual Award. Roger Statham undertook the initial planning, and worked with a small committee to arrange an inaugural award in 2005. In introducing the scheme, he wrote "NEPACS has been reflecting on these issues long and hard, and thinks that it is important now to reaffirm its values and its philosophy – after all NEPACS over 100 years ago, grew out of the attitude of Victorian society which was described as 'complacent, censorious and unimaginative'….It is that rehabilitative ideal that NEPACS now seeks to reassert, at the beginning of the twenty-first century, as a reminder that neither can we take these values for granted nor expect to see enough of them amongst the currency of everyday life".

The first year's awards went (a) to Del Stevens for the development in Northallerton Young Offenders Institution of an interactive Skills for Life programme, which aims to increase the confidence and self esteem of the under-achieving young men who so often find their way into prison; (b) to Julie McShane, a Probation Officer in Teesside for assiduous and caring work done with a serious offender, which represented the best of what can be achieved through one to one supervision, and was a reminder that people can be changed by people; and (c) to Neil Turver, Probation Officer in Kirklevington Prison who won a Lifetime Award, for thirty years of outstanding rehabilitative work with prisoners before discharge.

These set a pattern and a standard for future years. Other Awards have been received by people working in Probation for organizing a community service

NEPACS Awards 2009: Roberta Blackman-Woods MP for Durham *(5th from right, front row)* **with winners**

project to improve the physical environment of a neighbourhood, for setting up a supervision programme for arson offenders, and for carrying out an effective programme of debt counselling; and by a prison officer who by her own efforts transformed an area in the prison visits room into an attractive play place.

The scheme has gained in support and repute. The awards ceremony brings together a mixture of people working with offenders, in the best traditions of compassion, commitment and personal effort, to encourage them to 'turn round their lives', and uncovers facts about those who have been helped by disciplined but sensitive support to do just that. The ceremonies also provide occasions when many people at every level of the region's statutory and voluntary offender management initiatives meet each other, and consider the exciting work being done. The awards are presented by a person of repute, perhaps an M.P., who has an interest in penal reform.

The awards are both a way of saying 'thank you' and also a recognition and encouragement of work which promotes the rehabilitative ideal. "The purpose is to achieve benefits for society in general".

The Conferences

Our first conference was held in 1996, and, notwithstanding the fact that it was born of enthusiasm rather than experience, in the end it was very effective and much appreciated. Under the title, The Child and the Prison, it was the first national conference in Britain on the subject of children with parents in prison, and was held in Grey College, Durham. Our resources were slender, but we believed that we had something that needed to be said, and that we were qualified to present it. Roger Shaw, [69] Chief Probation Officer in Powys, who led the way in researching the situation and needs of prisoners' children, chaired the conference, with an opening address and guided the closing forum. David Philbrick, Child Psychiatrist with Durham Child and Mental Health Service, spoke on "Adolescent mental health and the prisoner's child" and Eva Lloyd, of Save the Children, on "Defending the rights of prisoners' children: principles and practice". Workshops were led by practitioners representing much of the pioneering work that was being done, including our own team on play projects in prisons. The findings were published, including a very stimulating paper on "Children coping with a father in prison: psychological tasks" by Anna Maria Pellegrini, who had

---

[69] Author of *Children of Imprisoned Fathers (1987), Prisoners' Children (1987)*, and a number of other titles on the same theme. He was the first to shed significant light by his research in Cambridge, into the numbers and situation of these children.

The Child & the Prison Conference, 1996.
Roger Shaw *(centre)* in the Chair

been invited to contribute, but with whom contact had been lost for a time. The small book was influential, and copies are still in demand. The conference was targeted at people involved with prisons, but also at those such as teachers, social workers, Health Visitors, who were working with the children of prisoners, and wanted more knowledge and support. There was a tremendous buzz at the conference, a great sense of relief at talking to each other, and motivation to go on with the work.

Eight years after this Jim Black suggested that NEPACS should once more engage in organizing conferences, perhaps on a two-yearly basis. Our conferences, he suggested, would be planned to raise and study critical issues within the criminal justice field, and would be worked out in relation to current topical research and our experience and practice. In planning them we should take account of international thinking and practice, and welcome the inclusion of scholarship, research and speakers from abroad. A small planning group and budget would be needed. The Board welcomed this proposal and agreed it. The new series began with a conference in April 2003 on Resettlement, responsibility and the individual, held in St Aidan's College. Our speakers gave thoughtful and stimulating papers. Professor David Wilson, Professor of Criminology, University of Central England on the theme of "responsibility and the individual", Mike Newell, Governor of HMP Durham on "responsibility and the statutory sector" and Roger Graef, Film and Documentary Producer and Director, on "responsibility and the community" opened up challenging issues about resettlement, and left us with unresolved questions to work on. The day was chaired skillfully by Anne Mace, Project Manager for the International Centre for Prison Studies and former Chief Probation Officer, West Yorkshire, who finally exhorted us "to learn from the many successes of resettlement, and to listen to all those involved, not least the offenders themselves, in a spirit of inclusiveness and reality". [70]

Our next conference, in 2005, was on the theme, "Prisoners and their families: sustaining the links". We wished to address the issue of the forces acting against prisoners' families' links in the face of all the evidence that sustaining those links is one of the most powerful forces supporting successful rehabilitation. We looked at other countries' approaches. Dr Ria Wolleswinkel of Maastricht University spoke on "Protection of family relations in law and practice" and Lloyd Withers, National Coordinator of the Canadian Families and Corrections Network on the "Strategic approach and policy to address the needs of the families of offenders", while Christine Knott, National Offender Manager spoke about official policy in this country. Together with a wide variety of workshops and the illuminating chairmanship of Mike Worthington, Visiting Professor of Community Safety, University of Northumbia, and retired Chief Probation Officer, Northumbria, the day provided a lively exploration of good insights into policy and practice, and some stimulating cross-fertilization of ideas.

---

[70] From Jim Black's account in the Annual Report.

For the fourth conference, we chose the neglected theme of the isolated prisoner, the one without family or friends to support him through the sentence and afterwards. We were aware of the large benefits to a prisoner of family support, the visits, the contacts with the free world, the supplements to the income and the gifts, and had some idea of the bleakness of life in prison without them. We were conscious of the support which the society provides to the families and friends, and so indirectly to the prisoners associated with them. We knew how little recognition is given to the needs of the isolated prisoners, and how greatly disadvantaged they are in the resettlement process in comparison with the rest. We hoped that attention might be drawn to this large group of prisoners, and that a fertile debate might take place.

The preparation began in 2007, but difficulty in identifying people sufficiently interested and informed in the subject confirmed our sense of the situation, and the conference was postponed until 2009.

The conferences honour our obligation to "collect and publish information relating to criminal justice matters and to the prevention of crime". They are immensely stimulating, and keep us in touch with policies, debate, development and with people everywhere who think and care about the criminal justice and those whom it affects.

The Volunteers [71]

We could not end without a thought about our volunteers. The society is well aware that they are the "core", the bedrock of the work, and they are no less valuable today than they were when there was no one else to do the work. Their contribution is not only that they provide a service which would not be affordable without them, but also the fact that they give their service to the visitors freely because they want to, and that they do so in a friendly way. The visitors who come to the centres and the other projects are important to them; their service is the first priority, and attention to friends, staff, officers, or anyone else takes second place. The visitors are treated with respect, the rooms are clean and attractive and decorated with flowers. This can mean a lot in lives where struggle, isolation, contempt are often encountered. The families of prisoners are usually at the bottom of the heap.

---

[71] See Appendix 5 for obituary of Joyce Mitchell, volunteer and Vice-President, whose contribution covered most of these 25 years.

Volunteers at Botanic Gardens Durham receive their long service certificates

The volunteers also provide a valuable link between the community and the prison world. "Coming from all age-groups, from many sectors of society, and from a widening geographical area, as they do, volunteers embody an involvement with, and of the local community which carries the influence of the Society, and understanding of the prison and the people connected with it, far beyond the walls of 22, Old Elvet". Roger Statham's words about the Society's coffee morning organized by the volunteers in 1988, "This was very much about the Society being part of the community" hint at an important aspect of the volunteers as bridging a formidable gap.

To a certain degree the volunteers are self-selected. By identifying themselves with what is often an unpopular cause, they have shown themselves to be non-judgmental and interested in people. Most find the work deeply interesting and rewarding, and many stay for a long time. Of the people who were with us at the beginning some have died in harness, and a few are still with us. The community of volunteers is strong. Beyond their rota duties, many support the fund-raising efforts, attend training sessions, come to parties, become Members of the Society, and show their support in other ways.

The fairly steady group of mature volunteers provides a solid base which students and other young people join from time to time. Some of the students remain for years, and are much affected by the experience. One has gone on to establish a children's project in her local prison, and one is now a trainee prison governor. I sometimes think that there are few activities in which people of all ages work together in such harmonious and mutually enriching ways.

From the start the volunteers were involved at every level, and it is still the same. Their opinions are valued and important in the running of the society, and a number of volunteers sit on the Board. Through careful communication – the diary, the Newsletter, the training events - we took pains to share our values. A volunteers' agreement established the obligations which a volunteer assumed and the corresponding rights to which they were entitled. This was expanded in the course of time into a handbook which laid out the ethos and values in the context of which NEPACS personnel carried out their duties.

The flexibility and resilience of the volunteers is well-known – witness their unflapping adjustment to life in the portacabins in 1997 (when the main building was hastily evacuated for urgent building repairs). The adjustment to the introduction of employed workers and the ongoing acceptance of the changing balance between paid and unpaid workers has not been easy. The

Society has acknowledged the stress: its steady insistence on the indispensability of both kinds of worker, and the value of each, has helped to support harmony and mutual respect. In the year 2009, we are still concerned to keep a beneficial balance, recognizing that the virtues of both voluntary and professional effort are considerable, and that for the best interests of prisoners, families, prisons and the community, both will play their part. Both groups share in project meetings, and training and fund-raising events, as well as in the tasks of the projects.

All of this, and the demanding nature of the duties with which they are entrusted, ensures that we attract volunteers with real ability and commitment and who make it possible to provide the high quality service at which we aim

"Each volunteer is someone who has decided to make a difference, to give time and energy to help and support others, She/he is also an ambassador for rehabilitation and gives the lie to "them and us". Elaine Lumley, Chief Officer, Teesside Probation, NEPACS Annual Report. 2005-06

....

End Note

Looking back at the start of this quarter century, it seems a very long time ago. Change in the criminal justice system has been rapid and far-reaching, and we have tried to keep abreast. Changes in our relationship with the Probation Service have resulted, but we still value the links and our working together in the key area of resettlement. [72] The profile of prisoners' families and visitors has become altogether clearer, and although things have gone up and down, their situation has been fundamentally changed. With the help of many people, connected with the Society and quite outside it, we have stood with the prisoners' families, have advocated for them and supplied help in a number of ways. It needed doing and it still does. We are aware, too, of other groups of people within our context who need and merit support, and we are ready to extend our vision. We have examined our structure and have taken steps which we hope will fit us for another period of useful work. As we look at our altered Society, we see one very different from last century's model, but, at the same time, we hope, very much the same in its humanity, values and purpose.

---

[72] *"Our partnership with NEPACS is a very good example of how the voluntary sector can add value to our core offending behaviour work. I hope that this will continue to grow". Jeff Fiddes, Partnership Manager, Northumbria Probation. "...in Probation's centenary year I would*

like to recognise and celebrate the very real achievements of colleagues in Probation and in NEPACS. We do help change lives and not everyone has the opportunity to do that!" Elaine Lumley, Chief Officer, Teesside Probation. NEPACS Annual Report, 2006-07

APPENDICES

1 - 6

APPENDIX 1. Date Chart

DATE	EVENTS IN NEPACS	PEOPLE	EVENTS OUTSIDE
Pre 1982	VC in 19 OE began; volunteers recruited Caravan & Grants projects	**Ruth Cranfield, Secretary** (1980-2005)	
1982	2nd century began	Jim Black, SPO, Co-opted committee member(1982-85)	
1983	First Training Day		*Forgotten Victims*, by Jill Matthews
1984	Caravan bigger, better facilities	Joan McArthur working for Caravan project	
1985	Small Home Office grant		Marked increase in prison population
1986	Visit to Winson Green VC HMP Frankland Play Project		
1987	Visitors'Centre in 22 Old Elvet		*Children of Imprisoned Fathers,*by Roger Shaw
1988	Fund-raising committee Publicity officer	**Roger Statham Chair**, (1988-94)	Conference at Bristol Changes in DHSS grants system made grants more difficult of access
1989			
1990	HMP Durham Play Project NEPACS *Bulletin* launched		FPFSG founded Strangeways riots,etc
1991	1st employee, Durham VC, part-time Second caravan added Booked visits began		Woolf Report introduces reforms All day visit, HMP Holloway Listener scheme started (Swansea)

1992	Durham Coordinator became full-time Support to Holme House and Low Newton visitors' centres planning		
1993	HMP Durham Special Children's Visits First Grants Policy		*"Prison works"* HO Circular 6/93 Agency status and de-volved budgets (PS)
1994		**John Howard,Chair**, **John Ayton, Acting Chair** (1994-95)	First Prison Ombudsman appointed Whitemoor escape
1995	1st payment re Frankland children's project NEPACS Review Group Caravan project moved to Cresswell Towers Childcare Worker apptd Frankland	**Brian Alport, Chair,** (1995-2005) **Peter Lucas, Treasurer** (1995-2005) **Donald Mackay,** **Grants Officer,** (1995-)	Parkhurst escape Incentives and Earned Privileges(IEP) scheme introduced Woodcock & Learmont Reports Setback for reform
1996	Grants policy revised 2nd caravan Conference: *"The Child & the Prison"*		x-ray machines introduced in prison search procedure
1997	Low Newton VC management adopted First Annual Training Day Probation withdraws from active support of caravan project Portacabin experience, Durham 1997-98 Representation on Home Office Family Ties Consultative Group	**Peter Warburton** Vice-Chair & Chair of PSC (1997-2001) Mark Kelly takes on site manage-ment of caravan scheme	
1998	Acklington & Castington VC managed Review Day Children's new conservatory playroom (DVC) opened Child/mother visits begun, Durham		Low Newton re-rolled to be a women's prison
1999	Consultation Day, April 17 FPFSG Youth Project, research phase Special children's visits, LN Revised Volunteers' Agreement Decrease in visits observed		Resettlement Pathfinder a pilot project Decrease in number of visits causing concern

2000	Youth Project pilot project Year 1, Research phase Play areas in Low Newton, Acklington Strapline adopted Consultation Day *(The Way Ahead)*		
2001	Incorporation as a Limited Company, 15th May 2001; new charity, NEPACS Young People's Project: pilot project, Youth Worker appointed Stakeholder pensions introduced Deerbolt children's project started Regional Play Work Manager apptd	**Jim Black Vice Chair** (2001-05)	National Probation Service established, focused on reducing reoffending Social Exclusion Unit, Reducing Offending by Ex-Prisoners
2002	NEPACS to manage the Frankland Visitors' Centre,1 April The North Eastern Prison After Care Society dissolved National Freephone Helpline for Prisoners' Families, NEPACS managing the NE sector NEPACS agreed to manage the Prison Tea Bars & a protracted taking-over process began		
2003	Regional Tea Bar Coordinator appt Risk assessment Pt time youth worker post at end of the Princess Diana scheme Conference: Resettlement, responsibility & the individual Award scheme adopted NEPACS to be subject of an MA anthropological research project Finance Officer post Operational Priorities Review Website fully established		
2004	Review of governance and structure: Future Directions.: redundancy of Manager's post NEPACS Awards scheme introduced		National Offender Management Service (NOMS) established closer working relationship between Prisons and Probation. Durham prison changed from Category A to being a Community Prison
2005	Play projects, Holme House and Castington Conference: Prisoners and their Families: Sustaining the Links First Awards Ceremony	**Jim Black Chairman** (2005-) **Trish McDonald Secretary** (2005-)	Security regulations escalated in work of the Tea Bars

2006	Strategy Meeting 27th March Greenside Educational Trust assets transferred to NEPACS	**Helen Attewell, Vice-Chair, Clive Constance,Treasurer** (2006-07)	Bromley Briefing prison factfile started (PRT)
2007	HMYOI Deerbolt, Visitors' Centre NEPACS Business Plan drawn up by Consultants Engagement with Families in Transition project (NOMS & GONE) Planning for conference on the isolated prisoner		Ministry of Justice established Corston Report on Vulnerable Women in Prison Centenary of the Probation Service

APPENDIX 2

The Communications Committee, 1999-2008

The Communications Committee, consisting of 5 Board members and a co-opted volunteer had 9 years of very active life.

Communication with the project users was advanced with the aid of a comment book on open display in each centre, in which the users were asked to make their comments, and the coordinator/manager responded. Questionnaires were also used and a number of leaflets updated. Of course, we continued to talk, as we had always done, with the visitors. A 'leaflet for the courts' was introduced in 2001, for distribution in the courts, carrying essential information for the families and friends of people who had just been sentenced to prison. It met an outstanding need for much neglected people, and was welcomed and displayed in Crown and magistrates courts in the region, and is updated regularly. (Attempts were made in vain to place it in police stations, and it could well have been used by solicitors.) Great attention continued to be given to the display of relevant information from other agencies.

For our staff and volunteers, copies of the Minutes of NEPACS meetings (apart from confidential matters) were made available in files, and the old organs of communication – the Volunteers' Newsletter, the diaries, the revised Handbook – nurtured. Events such as the Training Day, the Annual and Public Meetings, and social events, like the parties and the Underwater Odyssey (2004), not to mention the Coffee Mornings, brought volunteers, staff, and Board members together.

Reaching out into the community, a new leaflet of introductory information about NEPACS was planned and produced, relations with the press were cultivated – producing, for example, a cordial visit from Mike Amos of the Northern Echo followed by a lively article, the Bulletin was produced, a Speakers' Panel mobilized, with a file of speakers' notes, a NEPACS bookmark created, and the Durham city map persuaded to include both the Prison and the visitors' centre. A series of coffee mornings was arranged to introduce NEPACS to the community and possibly recruit some volunteers. In Durham, a series of At Homes was held for groups of people: local solicitors, clergy and chaplains, and the neighbourhood, with a view of getting to know each other better.

APPENDIX 3

THE VISITORS' CENTRES
principles and working standards
(from the Volunteers' Handbook)

1. The Visitors' Centres exist to meet the needs of adults and children visiting relatives or friends in prison. They aim to offer "a safe, pleasant environment where all visitors are met with dignity and respect, provided with the facilities they need and offered information, support and the opportunity to discuss the difficulties they may face in confidence" (Prison Service Guidelines, 1996). This statement sums up the basic principles underlying the NEPACS Visitors' Centres.

2. It follows that in the Centres the needs of the visitors come first. For them, the Visitors' Centre offers a threshold - a space between the prison and the outside world, where they may prepare, adjust, recover as they move between two very different environments. Volunteers should be sensitive and alert to their needs.

3. The fact that NEPACS is independent of the prison may make it easier to do this, and it may also be helpful to visitors who wish to discuss some of their concerns with centre personnel.

4. At the same time, NEPACS recognises that it has Service Level Agreements with the Prison Governors, and that it is essential to have good working relations with the prison and the prison staff if the centres are to work effectively.

5. NEPACS believes that by supporting visitors and providing appropriate facilities for them, a centre is also making significant contributions to prisoners and the prison.

6. All NEPACS workers should show courtesy and sensitivity in their dealings with everyone whom they encounter in the course of their duties.

7. One of the main needs of visitors is for information about visiting regulations and prison regimes, since ignorance increases their feeling of vulnerability and it is so hard for them to find out what they need to know. NEPACS centres therefore provide as much relevant, accurate, up-to-date information as they can, partly through notices, leaflets and handouts, and, more importantly, from centre staff. All volunteers should be sufficiently informed to answer frequently asked questions or to know where to seek help. However, no information should be offered unless it is known to be accurate.

8. Other information of value to visitors should be made available, e.g. about Assisted Prison Visits, travel, local accommodation, support agencies, other prisons to which their relative/friend may be being transferred.

9. The practical needs of visitors to the centre should be identified, and met wherever possible, even when this is not easy. For example, although the need of visitors to exchange notes for coins because of current prison regulations, creates a difficulty for centres, centre staff should try very hard to help.

10. NEPACS centres provide dedicated play space and equipment for children,, who are among our most important users, and need to feel welcome, safe and relaxed. All volunteers should be familiar with NEPACS Child Protection Policy and practice. I

11. NEPACS staff and volunteers should be friendly, non-judgmental, non-patronising, non-inquisitive, and at the same time sensitive, responsive and always willing to listen.

12. NEPACS centres have a policy of consulting their users, by whatever means possible, and treating all comments and suggestions seriously.

13. All NEPACS workers should understand and implement the Equal Opportunities Policy2 and be   committed to non-discriminatory practices.

14. All NEPACS workers should be aware of and implement Health & Safety procedures and policies.

15. All NEPACS workers must treat anything they may learn about individuals in the context of their work as confidential .

16. If complaints are made to Centre workers which relate to specific issues within the prison, the   visitor should be advised to use the prison complaints procedure and provided with an appropriate form if this is available. Staff should not act on behalf of the complainant. General issues raised, e.g. inability to make bookings, delays in process, etc., should be passed on through the coordinator to the designated prison liaison officer. A careful dated record should be made of any complaint related to issues at the centre, and this record given to the coordinator.

APPENDIX 4

<u>Members of the NEPACS Committee/Board</u>

Mr Brian Alport, 1996-2007
Ms Helen Attewell, 2005-07
Mr John Ayton, 1990-96
Mr K Barton, 1994
Mrs J. Brooks, -1984
Mr Clive Constance, 2006-
Mrs Ruth Cranfield, 1973-
Rev. Liz Cummings, 2006-
Miss B.Davis, -1984
Mr H. Davison, -1987
Mrs Thelma Denholm, -2000
Mrs Meta Dunn, 1989-2004
Mrs Betty Fawell, -1997
Ms Felicity Golton, -1982
Mr John Heron, -1992
Mr Howard, John, 1994
Mr J.W.P.Jackson, -1988
Mr Michael Larnach, 1993-99
Mr Cecil Laverick,1996-2007
Mr Peter Lucas, 1994-2005
Mr Donald Mackay, 1994-
Mr Tom Madrell, -2001
Miss E. Maughan, 1986-96
Mrs Margaret McDonald, -1990
Mrs Trish McDonald, 1991-
Miss Joyce Mitchell, 1986-2009
Mrs Kath Ogilvie, 1988-
Rev. G.B.Pattison, -1994
Ms Stella Perrott, 1989-94
Mr Jeffry Rackham, 1995-2004
Mrs Sonia Reed-Purvis, 1995-2004

Dr Fred Robinson, 1998-2007
Ms Yvonne Robson, 1991-94
Miss Kathy Scollen, -1996
Mrs Penny Scratchard, 1984-86
Mrs Sheila Seacroft, 1998-
Mrs Val Simpson, 1989-98
Mr Roger Statham,
1985-94, 2001-06
Mrs Wendy Statham, 2001-06
Mrs Margaret Stockdale, 2005-
Mrs Wendy Taylor, 1995-2006
Mrs Dorothy Terry, 1988-93
Mrs Sally Thompson, 1989-96
Mr J. Trueman, -1985
Mr Ian Tucker, 2004-
Mrs Audrey Vasey, 1995-2000
Rev. R. Wakefield, -1988
Mr Peter Warburton, 1997-2001
Mr Mark Weeding, 2005-
Mrs Kate West, 1987-91
Mr Mac Williams, 2004-07
Mrs Victoria Wood, 2004-06
Mrs Joanne Woods, 1994-2003

APPENDIX 5

Coordinators/Managers (1991-2007)

Joanne Woods, Coordinator, Durham Visitors' Centre 1991-92
Kathryn Nelson, Coordinator Durham Visitors' Centre 1992-95
Maureen Hindson, Coordinator/Manager Low Newton Visitors' Centre 1993-2005
June Diffey, Coordinator/Manager Durham Visitors' Centre 1995-2007
Ros Murray, Manager Low Newton Visitors' Centre 2004-
Laura Cockburn, Coordinator Acklington/Castington Visitors' Centre 1998-2003
Christine Blakey, NEPACS Manager 2001-05
Lynn Cowley, Youth Project Manager 2001-03
Christine Slassor, Regional Child Care Manager 2001-
Christine Lloyd, Regional Prisoners' Families Helpline Coordinator 2002-05
Debbie Flounders Coordinator/Manager Acklingron/Castington Visitors' Centre 2003-06
Christine Morris, Manager Acklington/Castington Visitors' Centre 2006-
Catherine Chesterton, Coordinator/Manager Frankland Visitors' Centre 2003-
Bev Thompson, Finance Officer 2003-09
Julie Barron, Regional Tea bar Coordinator/Manager Tea Bar Coordinator 2003-05
Sandy Anderson, Regional Tea Bar Coordinator/Manager 2005-
Kath Simpson, Administrator/ Office Manager 2007-
Jayne Turvill, Manager Deerbolt Visitors' Centre 2007-
Maggie Cherry, Manager Durham Visitors' Centre 2007-

APPENDIX 6

Joyce Mitchell 1915-2009 (whose contribution to NEPACS covered most of these 25 years)

Joyce had a great interest in life, in the natural world, in plants and animals. She loved poetry and was an avid reader. But most of all, she was interested in people. People who were in trouble specially interested her, and, recognizing a problem, she wanted to do something about it. This interest and desire to be involved set the pattern of her life. Her interest in speech therapy, which was in its early years as a profession, developed because she saw personal communication as so vital, and impairment of it as a great handicap in life. That led to her involvement with the code-breaking operation at Bletchley Park during the war, where training in speech patterns played an essential part. Afterwards, she returned to the speech therapy - in Oxford, Northern Ireland, and Newcastle, where she became a lecturer in the field and was awarded by the College of Speech Therapists for her "pioneering work with the elderly".

On her retirement, she looked round for some interesting and worthwhile occupation, tried NEPACS (which was just beginning its volunteer recruitment for a visitors' centre), liked what she found, and stayed. For a quarter of a century she made a rich contribution, as volunteer, critic, Board Member and, finally, Vice President. She began by becoming the Volunteers' Secretary, at the time when the volunteers did everything. She always engaged fully with whatever went on, supportive, constructive, probing into complacency (which was so often punctured by her quiet voice asking, 'Might I just say one thing?'), asking thoughtful questions, raising the stakes, insisting on high standards, testing, asking questions and overall encouraging. Most of all, she engaged with the people, with volunteers, staff, prison personnel, and especially with the visitors. Everyone was interesting to her, and she treated everyone with respect – which by no means prevented her from disagreement and argument with them. Her life was marked by warmth, humanity, uncommon good sense, and humour.

Joyce's was a benign and distinguished presence. Those of us who knew her will miss her greatly, and will remember, and be grateful for, her contribution and her influence in our second century's formative years.

Acronyms

APF   Action for Prisoners' Families

DHSS   Department of Health and Social Security

FPFSG   Federation of Prisoners' Families Support Groups

KidsVIP   Kids Visiting in Prison

NACRO   (National Association for the Care and Rehabilitation of Offenders)

NADPAS   National Association of Discharged Prisoners' Aid Societies

NAOPV   National association of Prison Visitors

NOMS   National Offender Management

PRT   Prison Reform Trust

Back cover image - Entrance to 19 Old Elvet